RENEWING
CHRISTIAN UNITY

RENEWING
CHRISTIAN UNITY

A Concise History of
the Christian Church (Disciples of Christ)

Mark G. Toulouse

Gary Holloway

Douglas A. Foster

Abilene Christian University Press

RENEWING CHRISTIAN UNITY
A Concise History of the Christian Church (Disciples of Christ)

Copyright 2011 by Mark G. Toulouse, Gary Holloway & Douglas A. Foster

ISBN 978-0-89112-543-3
LCCN 2010038753

Printed in the United States of America

LIBRARY OF CONGRESS CATALOGING-IN-PUBLICATION DATA
Toulouse, Mark G., 1952-
  Renewing Christian unity : a concise history of the Christian Church (Disciples of Christ) / Mark G. Toulouse, Gary Holloway, Douglas A. Foster.
    p. cm.
  ISBN 978-0-89112-543-3
  1. Christian Churches (Disciples of Christ)--History. 2. United States--Church history. I. Holloway, Gary, 1956- II. Foster, Douglas A. (Douglas Allen), 1952- III. Title.
  BX7316.T68 2010
  286.6'3--dc22

                                                                    2010038753

PHOTO CREDITS:
Pages 29, 31, 36,37, 47, 48, 49, 62, 68, 70, 80, 91, 93, 95, 103, 104, 105, 106, 115, 121, 127, 131, 132, 138, 140, 141, 146, 148, 154, 167, 169—From the collections of Disciples of Christ Historical Society, Nashville, Tennessee. Page 73—French artist Auguste Jean Hierveau's (1794-1880) India ink sketch of the Campbell-Owen debate, from Francis Trollope, Domestic Manners of the Americans. Page 110—Courtesy of Douglas Foster. Pages 116, 139—Courtesy of Mark Toulouse. Page 159—Courtesy of Ted Parks.

Cover design by Jeanette Munger
Interior text design by Sandy Armstrong

Abilene Christian University Press
1626 Campus Court
Abilene, Texas 79601

1-877-816-4455 toll free
For current information about all ACU Press titles, visit our Web site:
www.abilenechristianuniversitypress.com

10 11 12 13 14 15 / 7 6 5 4 3 2 1

*To Disciples congregations: each one, in its own way,
representative of the diversity in the midst of our unity*

CONTENTS

PREFACE

"Did Disciples of Christ really begin as a unity movement?"

"Disciples of Christ today believe and practice the same things we have from the beginning, don't we?"

"You can believe anything you want and still be a good member of the Disciples of Christ."

Statements like these by members of the Disciples reflect a serious lack of knowledge of our past and an increasing desire by many to know more of their heritage. This desire has led us to believe there is a need for a brief account of the history of the Christian Church (Disciples of Christ). This book hopes to serve newcomers and even long-time members of the church by giving them insights into our heritage. It also introduces this significant group of congregations to those unfamiliar with its place in American Christianity.

Any attempt to look at one's Christian ancestry is as pleasurable and painful as examining one's family tree. Some ancestors and family stories make us proud. Others we would just as soon forget. We are insiders to the Stone-Campbell movement who write with a deep appreciation for those who have gone before us. We would in no way bash the church of our ancestors. But as honest historians, we must present our story as we see it, "warts and all."

We do not consider the story of our past as merely interesting trivia—that's not what this book is about. Instead, we hope this work provides an accessible, informative, and helpful understanding of the past for Disciples. Some aspects of the tradition would be helpful to recover today as Disciples continue to seek ways to be faithful both to God and to the mission of the church.

This book has been a joint project in every way. As we worked on this book together, we have learned the difficulties and the joys of Christian unity. We have not always agreed, but we have always been willing to discuss. This seems to us the basis for more than writing together. It reflects the attitude toward Christian unity modeled by the early leaders discussed in this book.

Since the first volume of this series, the premier reference work on Stone-Campbell history has been published: *The Encyclopedia of the Stone-Campbell Movement*, edited by Paul Blowers, Douglas Foster, and D. Newell Williams (Eerdmans, 2005). The articles are engaging as well as informative, and reading appropriate articles in the *Encyclopedia* alongside your reading in this book will enhance your enjoyment and understanding of this material.

Our thanks to John Knight for preparing the index for this book.

DISCIPLES AND HISTORY

He came into the first class session for Disciples History and Theology and announced, "I really don't care what Barton Stone or Alexander Campbell said. The theology of the nineteenth century has very little to say to the church of the twenty-first century." Or take another example. A seminary student, serving as a guest preacher in a small rural congregation one Sunday, met the chair of deacons after worship. The good deacon asked her, "What are you studying this semester?" She answered, "New Testament, Introduction to Theology, Christian Ethics, and Disciples History and Theology." "Disciples History and Theology?" the deacon replied. "Are they teaching you just how far Disciples have fallen away from the practices of the early church?"

These stories illustrate that many in the church possess a rather jaded view of the value of history. In the first instance, the student is confident that the future is always better than the past. There are many people in North America, for example, who believe history is naturally progressive in nature. Things only get better with time. They would be inclined to use contemporary standards, the norms, say, of the twenty-first century to judge the actions of people in the nineteenth century. But this constitutes an abuse of history. All they are doing is reading their contemporary beliefs into the past. They see what they want to see and are surprised by nothing. They take pride in believing they are smarter than anybody in the past because knowledge has grown with time. Besides, they have easy access to CNN, the *New York Times*, and, the preference of contemporary students, Facebook and Twitter.

Is "later in time" always better? Or do such attitudes tend toward the self-righteous? When one looks at history with this perspective, one can learn very little from it. That is too bad, because historical understanding helps us to see ourselves through a different lens. It enables us to encounter people who are both like us and different from us at the same time. History helps us to understand just how bound by our own cultural contexts we tend to be in the modern world.

The second illustration above is representative of some Disciples who believe that history is one continual downward spiral. This approach to history is opposite to that of the student entering his first class. Everything in the past is automatically better than everything in the present. The world, through time, only gets worse. Wisdom resides in the past, not in the present. For many Disciples, the appearance of Christ is the exceptional point in history, the only highpoint. Everything else is decline. Thus, the closer your Christian faith is to the faith of the earliest Christians, the better Christian you are. As the church has moved through history, it has only fallen into lower levels of degradation and disgrace. The Campbells, Barton Stone, Walter Scott, and other founders of Disciples life, these folks argue, knew that. This is why they sought to "restore" in their time the faith and church life of the earliest Christians. Though this approach might free some of those who believe in it from a captivity to the wiles of modern culture, it only traps them in the cultural perspectives of an earlier time.

Both of these attitudes represent an abuse of history. Neither understands history as it develops. Both are judgmental of all historical action, whether by using contemporary standards or those of the past. To understand history and its significance today, we must seek to understand the lives and work of those in the past from the perspective of their present. This book attempts to understand the past, not from a bias for either the present or the past, but from a genuine desire to understand how the history of Disciples unfolded within time. How did Disciples encounter and respond to the contemporary forces surrounding them as they sought to be faithful to God?

MANY BIRTHDAYS

We understand those who want to deny the effects of history. On the side of the church building where one of us grew up were the

12

words: "Church of Christ, Established 33 A.D." The idea expressed the hope of the congregation as it worked to be like the church of the New Testament, the one established at Pentecost. That ideal still burns brightly in the hearts of many. Disciples do not want to restore everything about the early church (no one wants to be exactly like the Corinthians), but many do want to be the kind of church that the first-century churches should have been. In a real sense, Disciples can trace their own history as church to Pentecost.

But do Disciples have a history after Pentecost? Honesty requires that we answer, "Yes." The whole history of the church, as messy and fallen as it has been, is in some sense our history. Although we may want to be like the early church in some respects, we must admit that we are not the first Christians. More than two thousand years have passed. Previous generations have handed Christian faith on to us. We would not have the Bible itself were it not for the faithful labors of copyists and translators. One reason for studying Christian history is to honor all those who have sought to be faithful in their own time and place.

History also helps contemporary Disciples understand how faithful Christians in the past struggled to follow God in their own context. If we can see how the church in the past often conformed too much to its culture, then perhaps we can see how our own culture threatens the current church. Studying history also enables us to understand those ways the church affected the culture around it in positive ways.

Studying history can also help contemporary Christians to understand the Bible. Disciples, historically, are a people of the book. Those who lived before us taught the generations following the importance of reading it and attempting to live according to the principles found within it. By seeing how previous generations understood (and misunderstood) the Bible, we gain a perspective on its meaning for our time.

This book focuses on Disciples history in the context of North America. While it is true in one sense that Pentecost is the church's birthday, there are other dates we can point to as beginning points of the existence of Disciples of Christ in the United States. The first "founding document" of Disciples history is *The Last Will and Testament of the Springfield Presbytery* written in 1804. The ministers who wrote those words began the first group of independent churches in this movement. Although many before him called Christians back to the Bible for the sake of Christian unity, Thomas Campbell's publication of *The Declaration and Address* in 1809 marked a significant intellectual beginning for Disciples. The Disciples of Christ understand this date as their starting point (see Chapter Four), celebrating their centennial in 1909 and their bicentennial in 2009.

At the end of the nineteenth century, the movement divided with the Disciples of Christ and Churches of Christ becoming separate groups. Some place that division in 1889, when Daniel Sommer and others called for a break of fellowship in the "Address and Declaration" at Sand Creek, Illinois. The "official" date of that division is 1906 (see Chapters Eight and Nine). Thus, in one sense, Churches of Christ in America marked their centennial in 2006.

So what is the birth date of Disciples? All and none of the above. Disciples do want to be the church founded at Pentecost. Yet, we must also admit that we are one representation of the church, one among many, in a North American context. We owe our identity to Thomas Campbell, Alexander Campbell, Barton Stone, and others in the nineteenth century. We also owe a debt to those who lived in the centuries between the first and the nineteenth, those who shaped the nature of church life during their centuries. We learn both from their mistakes and from their successes. And, since the nineteenth, on into the twenty-first century, Disciples are formed in their identity as Christians by both those who have sought to be faithful as Disciples of Christ and those many other Christians with whom Disciples have sought unity over these more than two hundred years.

TRADITION AND TRADITIONALISM

Both the student and the deacon mentioned above also reflect a long-standing opposition to tradition. Why should Disciples study history if we have always been against tradition? The answer to this question lies in the distinction between "tradition" and "traditionalism." Historian Jaroslav Pelikan has defined tradition as "the living faith of the dead" and traditionalism as "the dead faith of the living."

The Bible is both positive and negative about tradition (the biblical word means simply "something passed down"). When tradition becomes traditionalism, that is, when human beings become set in their ways regardless of the message of the gospel, then it deserves condemnation. Both Jesus (Matthew 15:1-6) and Paul (Colossians 2:8) condemn human traditions that supersede the will of God. On the other hand, Paul many times urges the churches to "hold on to the traditions" he had taught them (I Corinthians 11:2; 2 Thessalonians 2:15; 3:6). In Paul's view, these were not human traditions, but rather represented the will of God. Of course, many who are stuck in traditionalism make the same claim.

Why study the history of Disciples? It is one way churches can honor those Christians who struggled to pass the tradition of faith on to those of us who came after them. Yet, those traditions must always be viewed in light of our best attempts, as a community, to understand both the Bible and the nature of faith. Indeed, for Disciples, one of the strongest traditions is the one that stresses the gospel: the good news proclaiming, as Clark Williamson describes it, the love of God for each and every human being and all the world, a love that also inherently demands that justice be provided for each and every one (and all the world) whom God loves. Christians find the clearest expression of this gospel in Christ, but also in the stories of God's dealings with and activities through both Israel and the church. The narratives of the Bible cover it all.

This is why Disciples have valued the testimony of the Bible over the myriad of claims often found within tradition. Nevertheless, responsible traditions are necessary to give shape to church life and to help in passing on the faith. Indeed, church traditions are inevitable. The alternative would be starting the church over anew each day, resulting in chaos. Traditions become harmful only when they exist as fixed traditionalism, something that often replaces the message of grace so clearly contained in the gospel.

Denying Disciples have a history often results in Disciples being captive to it. By being blind to the historical forces that shape the church's practices, Disciples occasionally fall prey to confusing their conclusions with the will of God. By denying Disciples have a history, they become traditionalists who too easily assume that their very human beliefs came directly from God.

We write this brief history as Christians identified with the Stone-Campbell Movement. We appreciate its history, but are also mindful of its weaknesses. If we neglect understanding the good

15

that generations before us accomplished as church, we become both ungrateful and ignorant. If we ignore their mistakes, we become traditionalists who prize our own human history above our need to hear and heed the gospel. Only by taking an honest look at who we have been can we understand who we are. By the grace of God, human beings possess the ability to think historically and to grow in our understanding through using that ability wisely. Thinking historically is an important part of our ability to be faithful to God in our own time and place.

In the remaining paragraphs of this chapter, we offer a brief synopsis of nineteen centuries of the history of the church. Many fine works are available that treat this history in detail, and, if possible, readers should seek them out to gain a better picture of the vast changes experienced by the church during these years. What follows here only teases out a few themes or characteristics of these periods in the history of Christianity. The reason we address these periods at all, though by necessity all too briefly, is simply to make the point that they do bear, in some important ways, upon the history and beliefs eventually found within the Stone-Campbell Movement.

THE EARLY AND MEDIEVAL CHURCH

Acts 2 portrays the first church in Jerusalem as a model church. Members listened to the apostles, prayed, shared their food and money, grew numerically, and experienced harmony with those around them (Acts 2:42-47). The rest of Acts and the New Testament, however, make it clear that the first-century church had its problems. Individual congregations like Corinth faced divisions. The Judaizers claimed another way of salvation (Galatians 1:6-9). Others claimed a special knowledge unavailable to most (Colossians 2:16-23). Some claimed to be Christians while denying that Jesus had lived as a human being (2 John 7). Even in the best of churches, there were those who did not get along (Philippians 4:2). The biblical witness clearly describes a diverse church.

Thus, from the beginning church history has been messy. On the one hand, the church seeks to serve divine purposes in history, in that it was born in the wake of Christ's witness and example. On the other, it consists of redeemed people who are still human, flawed, and fallen. Although Jesus prayed that believers would have unity (John 17:20-23), from the very beginning of the church that unity has been a struggle. The unity found within the earliest church always existed in spite of both the human weaknesses attached to it and the diversity in belief and intention found in congregations associated with it.

During the beginning years of the church, the apostles were there to give guidance and direction. Their teaching and writings provided shape and unity for the churches. This is why the founders of the Stone-Campbell Movement referred to the first-century church as a model. The church was not a perfect church, but it was largely faithful. By the second century, however, the apostles were gone. The books of the New Testament existed, but the church had not yet collected and recognized them as scripture (that process happened slowly over the next several centuries). One force that continued to give the church cohesion was the persecution of Christians by the Roman Empire. Although the persecution was sporadic and usually local, it did tend to limit membership to the fully committed. One did not become a Christian to get ahead in society. Membership could mean death. The examples of martyrs provided courage for the church.

Everything changed by the beginning of the fourth century. A new emperor, Constantine (born around 272 and died in 337), won his crown in battle after appealing to the Christian God. Although he tried to please both pagans and Christians as emperor, he eventually became a Christian and began the process of transforming Christianity into the state religion.

Obviously some good resulted from Constantine's decision. The government no longer jailed, tortured, and killed Christians. The empire eventually ended slavery and protected human rights. However, the power structure of the empire quickly tended to dominate the church. Some leaders in the church became self-interested and sought their own avenues of power, while others sought to maintain faith in the midst of cultural struggles and counter forces. Like every era of church life, both leaders and members represented a mixed bag containing both selfish human intentions and faithful efforts to represent the meaning of the gospel. Over several centuries, the medieval Roman Catholic Church also developed an elaborate system of penance that included belief in purgatory, the intercession of saints, and the power of the priest to absolve persons from the punishment of their sins.

In spite of developments away from the simplicity of the New Testament witness, Christians owe a considerable debt to everyday members of the medieval church. Christians during those years continued to pass along the gospel story. They preserved the manuscripts of both the Old and New Testaments and sought to preserve the church. But they also made mistakes, some of them tragic and corrupt (the Crusades, for example). Yet the work and witness of the church somehow, perhaps against all odds, survived the worst of those mistakes. And the witness and heirs of those who did not survive the purges of a crusading church still rightfully demand repentance from the heirs of a church that had lost its way.

The Reformation

Even during the medieval period, some attempted to reform the church, with varying degrees of success. By the sixteenth century, many more wanted reform, including Martin Luther (1483-1546), a German monk and theologian. The heart of his own Catholic theology was justification by grace through faith, in contrast to many popular practices of his day that implied people could earn salvation through specific actions. Luther also called the church back to the authority of the Bible, claiming *sola scriptura*, "scripture alone" as

Martin Luther   John Calvin

Anabaptist Martyrs

his guide. He never intended to form a new church, but eventually his followers formed a separate body.

In Switzerland, a more thoroughgoing Reformation took place under Huldreich Zwingli (1484-1531) at Zurich. Though his career was brief, Zwingli began the "Reformed" tradition, the second major Protestant movement after Lutheranism. John Calvin (1509-1564) in Geneva later became the chief influence in this Reformed Church. Calvin's emphasis on the sovereignty of God led him to emphasize the doctrine of predestination. Lingering elements of this doctrine still shape some churches of the Reformed tradition, especially among more conservative Presbyterians and Baptists.

A third branch of the Reformation was the Anabaptist or Radical Reformation. Some considered these Christians "radical" because they insisted on a stricter return to the teaching of the New Testament, many believing the pacifism Jesus taught in the Sermon on the Mount was central to the Christian life. They also insisted on believer's baptism, thus earning themselves the name Anabaptists ("rebaptizers") from those who practiced infant baptism. This also meant a break with the union of church and state that Constantine had established centuries before. Almost every government in Europe, whether Catholic or Protestant, viewed the Anabaptist refusal to baptize infants as a threat to the social order. Consequently, they faced severe persecution. Since most of them were pacifists, they refused to use violence in their efforts to resist the government. Consequently, many fled to Holland where there was some degree of religious tolerance.

The Stone-Campbell Movement owes a great debt to the Reformation. Barton Stone, Alexander Campbell, and other early leaders often praised Luther and Calvin, and other reformers, for their work in leading people back to the Bible and a renewed appreciation of God's grace. Indeed, they saw their task as finishing the work of Reformation begun by Luther and others, often calling their work, "the Current Reformation." Disciples were particularly influenced in their views of both baptism and the Lord's Supper (see Chapter Seven) by their dependence on Reformed theology.

ENGLAND AND SCOTLAND

Since most of the early settlers in Britain's North American colonies came from England and Scotland, the reformation in those countries had a more direct effect on the founders of the Stone-Campbell Movement. In England, prompted by personal, political, and religious problems, King Henry VIII (1491-1547) broke from the Roman Catholic Church in 1534 to form the Church of England. Of all the Reformation churches, this Anglican Church made the fewest changes from Catholic practices.

Consequently, leaders arose who, influenced by the Reformed teaching of John Calvin, desired more reform in the Church of England. Their attempt to purify the church led to their being called Puritans. Some despaired of ever changing the Church of England and separated from it to form their own churches. These Separatists faced persecution in England and so some fled to Holland, then to America, becoming the Pilgrims of Plymouth Plantation.

Other Separatists organized themselves under groups of elders or presbyters. Through the leadership of John Knox (1513-1572) in Scotland, this Presbyterian system became the official Church of Scotland. Still other Separatists in England began to practice believer's immersion, and so became known as Baptists.

Members of all these groups—Anglicans, Puritans, Separatists, Presbyterians, and Baptists—eventually migrated to the English colonies in North America. Thus, as we will see in the next chapter, the variety of churches in North America soon led to a unique religious situation.

ENLIGHTENMENT RATIONALISM

One of the consequences of both the Protestant and Catholic Reformations during the sixteenth and seventeenth centuries was a series of religious wars in Europe. The treaty that ended the bloody Thirty-Years War in 1648, the Peace of Westphalia, decreed that the religion of a territory's leader determined the religion of the territory. There were Catholic countries and Protestant countries with little toleration for religious dissent. Consequently, wars over religion continued to rage throughout Europe for decades. Some responded to the religious wars between Protestants and Catholics in Europe by demanding a more reasonable religion, one that would not lead to bloodshed. Some even rejected all religion as unreasonable. Others believed religion became reasonable only when it understood itself as a part of the natural order of things; religion always became unreasonable when it claimed miraculous connections. Generally known as Deists, these Christians sought to redefine Christianity by cleansing it of its dependence on the supernatural. All these approaches to religion contributed to the emergence of the Enlightenment era or Age of Reason in the seventeenth and eighteenth centuries.

In the midst of these developing arguments about the nature of religion, still others argued that Christianity could be defined by both the supernatural and the reasonable. Among these thinkers, John Locke (1632-1704) became the most influential. He argued that all human ideas result from experience and in light of experience, the essence of Christianity—Jesus as the Messiah—could be understood as eminently reasonable.

John Locke

21

Locke understood the supernatural as above reason, but never contrary to it. Thus, supernatural claims could never be unreasonable, when understood in light of human experience.

All of these forms of Enlightenment thought found their way to North America. Deism influenced the American founders, such as Thomas Jefferson who produced a New Testament completely stripped of miracle stories. More important to Disciples, the Stone-Campbell Movement was born in an era when both the rationalism of John Locke and the pietism emerging from the Second Great Awakening (emerging in 1801) heavily influenced all of its early leaders.

This brief survey of church history in the western world before the colonization of North America reminds us that Christianity has a long history. As much as contemporary Christians might disagree with the centuries of Christians who came before them, they must admit they are in one sense related to them. They all sought to find ways to serve God appropriate to their time and place. And like those who followed, they did so as human beings who represented all that being human means. The new religious situation in America, however, provided the soil for even more new ideas, and a prevailing, often naïve, belief in innocence and the possibility for greater reform helped create even more new forms of church life.

FOR FURTHER READING

Garrett, Leroy. *The Stone-Campbell Movement*. Joplin, Mo.: College Press, 2002. See pages 21-45.

Gonzalez, Justo L. *The Story of Christianity*. New York: HarperCollins Publishers, 2010.

Williamson, Clark M. *Way of Blessing, Way of Life*. St. Louis: Chalice Press, 1999. See pages 73-97.

QUESTIONS FOR DISCUSSION

1. What are two problematic approaches to history often found among Disciples?

2. List some of the benefits of thinking historically.

3. What is the difference between tradition and traditionalism? Give some biblical examples of the difference.

4. What are some of the debts we owe to the early church? The medieval church? The Reformation? What lessons can we learn today from the church in those times?

5. Is Christianity a "reasonable" religion? What is an appropriate relationship between the "reasonable" and the "spiritual" for human beings?

THE IDEA OF RESTORATION IN THE EARLY UNITED STATES

Why is the practice of religion in the United States different from that found in Europe and other parts of the world? Why is it, even today, that there are more denominations in the United States than in other countries across the world? Why is the percentage of regular churchgoers higher in the United States (though this percentage seems to be falling annually)?

We find the answer to all these questions in the country's early history. That history also provided the soil that gave birth to the Disciples of Christ. Although nine of the thirteen colonies had "establishments"—tax-supported Christian churches—a new situation developed in the colonies that had never existed before. No single Christian group became dominant over all the colonies. The Puritans dominated New England, but there were also small numbers of Baptists, Anglicans, Quakers, Deists, Lutherans, Catholics, and Unitarians there. The Anglicans were most numerous in the southern colonies, but all manner of dissenters were also found there. The middle colonies had accumulated the largest numbers of Christian diversity, representing in significant numbers a variety of Christian expressions. And, of course, non-Christian religion also existed, including, for example, Judaism and a wide variety of Native American spirituality.

Consequently, no one Christian denomination could be *the* church of the colonies. We take that situation for granted, but it was unique for its time. In Europe, every country had an official state religion, with (at best) limited tolerance for other religious groups.

For example, English authorities jailed the Separatist Puritans that Americans call the "Pilgrims" for preaching against the Church of England. Therefore, they left England for the Netherlands and eventually came to North America, not to find the religious freedom we have today, but to have the freedom to set up "the true church." They were no more tolerant of Quakers and Baptists than the English authorities had been tolerant of Puritans. Yet the vast diversity of Christian expression in the colonies virtually guaranteed the expansion of religious freedom.

A New View of Religious Freedom

Since no religious group dominated all the colonies, a new form of religious freedom began. It included an emphasis on freedom from church or clerical authority. Many colonists, especially on the frontier, wanted no part of a pope, a bishop, or even a group of clergy making rules for the church. Instead, they longed for a more democratic form of government where ordinary members made collective decisions for the church. This desire for religious democracy also produced a new form of minister—one who was not formally educated, but who came from the people—in contrast to the traditional elite, educated ministry.

New leaders emphasized a freedom from tradition. The common sense of the people replaced the rulings of popes and councils, the historic creeds, and the writings of educated theologians. People increasingly believed they should read the Bible for themselves and think for themselves, and not trust the clergy to do their thinking for them.

Because of this democratization of Christianity, another freedom arose—the freedom to begin new churches. What happened if your reading of scripture differed significantly from the teaching of your church? If you could not persuade your church to change, then there was no choice left but to form your own "true" church. As a result, dozens of upstart churches began and prospered in the emerging United States, the Baptists and Methodists in particular, many outgrowing the more established churches. After a while those newer churches themselves resisted change in their practices and grew to be leaders in the larger culture. Consequently, some in those groups rebelled against their tradition and formed still other religious sects.

A New View of Religious Authority

Because of this freedom, many thought it no longer necessary for religious authority to come from a recognized hierarchy, creeds, or an educated clergy. Instead authority became truly democratic, a rule of the people. The Reformation principle of *sola scriptura* (scripture alone) evolved into the idea that each Christian was her or his own interpreter of the Bible.

This interpretation arose in the context of rationalism and common sense philosophy. A great confidence arose that human beings could simply "reason" their way to truth. The truth of any religious teaching became subject to reason. Increasingly, in Christian circles, this meant that each individual had the right and responsibility to read scripture and interpret it. Personal experience also shaped this rationalism, particularly on the frontier. In other words, in some locations, true religion was to be heart-felt and mysterious, while at the same time being reasonable to the average person.

Ironically, this rejection of traditional religious authorities gave power to another elite, the religious demagogues. Although theoretically each person was a Bible interpreter, in fact a religious leader who could move an audience had tremendous influence on how that audience read scripture. This accounts for the rise of popular preaching in the language of the people. It also explains the popularity of the new religious press. By publishing a paper, preachers could influence thousands to see the Bible and the church their way. Popular hymns also shaped the theology of the people.

Christians largely rejected traditional religious authority to appeal to the authority of personal interpretation of scripture. Ironically, this left them with the uncertain authority of popular preachers and mass movements. Denominations multiplied. The church seemed less unified. Religious truth became a product of the people in a destructive way. Over time, for some, the size of the church determined the truth of its teaching. Popularity equaled truth. Some measured success in numbers, not in faithfulness. Too often, freedom to interpret the Bible for one's self became bondage to self-promoting preachers who could sway the most people.

A CALL FOR RESTORATION

This was the setting for the birth of the Disciples. Many were looking for a more certain authority in religion. Many wondered why there were so many denominations and which (if any) was the true church. The scandal of division among Christians was evident on the frontier. A small settlement of a hundred people might have three or more struggling churches, often in constant conflict with each other over which one was the true, correct church.

But the frontier also offered many religious leaders the freedom to rethink the shape of the church. Independently, many of them decided that a return to the Bible and the church of the New Testament offered the best hope of having a faithful and a unified church in their new American setting. These "back to the Bible" movements grew up in several denominations in various parts of the frontier.

As we saw in Chapter One, the dream of going "back to the Bible" did not begin in the eighteenth-century in North America. The Renaissance call to go "back to the sources" led many like the Roman Catholic scholar Erasmus (1466-1536) to emphasize the importance of going to the New Testament for guidance and authority. As we have seen, the Reformation had its motto of *sola scriptura*, scripture alone. The Puritans in England and the early New England colonies wanted their churches to resemble closely the biblical model. However, on the eighteenth-century frontier, many called for a more thorough reformation of the church. Some used the word "restoration" for this reform.

"Restoration" was a more popular term in the Campbell Movement (see Chapter Four) than in the early movements examined in this chapter, but the concept of restoration was common to all these groups. What did they mean by a "Restoration Movement"?

Some thought of restoration in terms of restoring a house. Restoring the church was not building from scratch; it's not as though the church had completely disappeared, but it had deteriorated through the years and needed to be restored to its original state. Think of restoring an old house. Essential portions of the house may be sound and original—the foundation and plumbing, for example—while other portions need replacing. Restoration means removing newer additions and restoring older sections in order to return the house to its original condition.

This was the goal of all the groups in this chapter. What most also had in common was agreement on the purpose of restoration. For many, to be the pure church of the Bible was not an end in itself. The purpose of restoring the church was to reach the unity among Christians that Christ prayed for: "That all of them may be one . . ." (John 17:21). Although there were significant differences among these groups, they all called Christians back to the Bible to restore to the church certain things they believed it had lost.

CHRISTIANS OF THE SOUTH: JAMES O'KELLY

"I am for Bible government, Christian equality, and the Christian name," said James O'Kelly (1735-1826), an early Methodist preacher in North Carolina and Virginia. When the Methodist church organized itself in Baltimore in 1784, O'Kelly and a few other ministers questioned the appointment of Francis Asbury as one of two superintendents of the church. They believed Asbury, who began to call himself bishop, held too much power over the churches. Eventually, O'Kelly not only opposed Asbury but the whole idea of a bishop who appoints ministers in each church. Instead, he felt each congregation should act democratically, like a republic, to govern its own affairs.

In 1793, O'Kelly and others broke from Asbury's leadership, calling themselves Republican Methodists. In August 1794, the leaders of this group met and went one step farther. They decided to call themselves "Christians" to the exclusion of other names and take the Bible alone as their creed. Eventually, they adopted six "Cardinal Principles of the Christian Church":

James O'Kelly

29

1. The Lord Jesus Christ is the only Head of the Church.
2. The name Christian should be used to the exclusion of all party and sectarian names.
3. The Holy Bible, or scriptures of the Old and New Testaments, is our only creed, and a sufficient rule of faith and practice.
4. Christian character, or vital piety, is the only test of church fellowship and membership.
5. The right of private judgment and the liberty of conscience are the privilege and duty of all.
6. The union of all followers of Christ to the end that the world may believe.

These leaders did not intend these items as a formal creed (since item three rejects creeds), but these propositions do express the basic outlook of the O'Kelly group and of all the restoration movements on the frontier. Note that even Christian unity was not an end in itself, but should result in bringing the gospel to the world.

These Christian churches eventually numbered ten thousand or so members in North Carolina and Virginia. Some of these congregations eventually adopted believer's immersion and united with the New England Christians in the early 1800s (see below). Others maintained infant baptism and rejoined the Methodists in 1934. Others joined with the Stone "Christians" (see Chapter Three). One connection between the O'Kelly and the Stone Movement was the work of Rice Haggard (1769-1819) who convinced both groups to take the name "Christian" to the exclusion of more divisive names.

THE NEW ENGLAND CHRISTIAN CONNECTION: JONES AND SMITH

Independently a similar movement arose among Baptists in New England. At this time, Baptists were strongly Calvinistic, believing that God predestined some and not others to be Christians. Abner Jones (1772-1841), a physician and preacher in Vermont joined with like-minded Baptists in denying Calvinism and taking the name Christian. They organized a Christian church in Lyndon, Vermont, in 1801. Jones became a traveling evangelist, spreading the message of non-creedal Christianity.

In 1803, Jones first met Elias Smith (1769-1846), another Baptist minister who had formed a Christian congregation the previous year in Portsmouth, New Hampshire. Smith was a fiery proponent of religious freedom who published one of the earliest Christian papers in America, the *Herald of Gospel Liberty* (begun in 1808). He also popularized his ideas through hymns that attacked the prevailing religious authorities. Jones and Smith combined their efforts and by 1807 had established fourteen congregations of Christians in New England.

Elias Smith

The Smith-Jones Movement was so insistent on doctrinal diversity that eventually it splintered and disappeared as a separate fellowship. Some became Unitarians. Many later joined the Adventists. Some joined with the O'Kelly Christians in the South and the Stone Movement to form the Christian Connection. In 1931, the congregations of the Connection that had not merged with the Campbell Movement in the nineteenth century became part of the Congregational Christian Church which in turn merged in 1957 with the Evangelical and Reformed Church to form the United Church of Christ.

The freedom of the frontier thus produced two Christian "restoration" movements, one from the Methodists and one from the Baptists. It was to produce two more from a Presbyterian background.

For Further Reading

Conkin, Paul K. *American Originals: Homemade Varieties of Christianity*. Chapel Hill: University of North Carolina Press, 1997. See pages 1-8.

Cummins, D. Duane. *The Disciples: A Struggle for Reformation*. St. Louis: Chalice Press, 2009. See pages 1-22.

Garrett, Leroy. *The Stone-Campbell Movement*. Joplin, Mo.: College Press, 1994. See pages 47-70.

Hatch, Nathan O. *The Democratization of American Christianity*. New Haven: Yale University Press, 1989.

Hughes, Richard T. and C. Leonard Allen. *Illusions of Innocence: Protestant Primitivism in America, 1630-1875*. 1988; reprint edition, Abilene: Abilene Christian University Press, 2008.

Mead, Sidney E. *The Lively Experiment: The Shaping of Christianity in America*. 1963; reprint edition, Oregon: Wipf and Stock Publishers, 2007.

Toulouse, Mark G. *Joined in Discipleship: The Shaping of Contemporary Disciples Identity*. St. Louis: Chalice Press, 1997. See pages 55-72.

Questions for Discussion

1. What factors led to religious freedom in the United States? How does that freedom help explain the unique aspects of American religion?

2. Why are there so many different churches in North America? Why have new religious groups been so popular in the United States?

3. What do you first think of when you hear "Restoration Movement"? How have many within Disciples understood restoration? What do you think is the most appropriate way to understand it?

4. Is Christian unity still a noble goal to pursue? What would that unity look like?

5. Are the "six points" of the O'Kelly Christians a good summary of what the church should be? What would you add or subtract from their list?

6. What did the Smith-Jones New England Christians and the O'Kelly Christians have in common? How were they different? Is there anything we can learn today from these two groups?

CHAPTER 3

BARTON STONE AND CHRISTIAN UNITY

Although there were groups of "Christians" in the South and in New England, the most numerous band grew out of the Presbyterian and Baptist churches in Kentucky and Tennessee. The leader of these "Christians of the West" was a deeply pious man named Barton W. Stone (1772-1844).

STONE'S EARLY LIFE

Born in Maryland, Barton W. Stone grew up initially as a nominal Episcopalian. In 1779, after the death of his father, he moved with his family to Virginia. During his teen years, he attended Baptist and Methodist churches, but could not experience the kind of dramatic conversion some did. Instead, he decided to improve his position in society by continuing his education and becoming a lawyer.

He enrolled in a "log college" (a typical, one-teacher frontier school) run by David Caldwell (1725-1824), a Presbyterian minister in North Carolina. Under his influence and the preaching of revivalist James McGready (1760-1817), Stone had a conversion experience, became a Presbyterian, and believed himself called by God to preach. Finishing his studies with Caldwell in three years, Stone was among the most educated persons on the American frontier.

Before the Presbyterians ordained him, Stone had many internal struggles. He questioned the depth of his conversion, the genuineness of his call to preach, and the truth of the traditional doctrines of the Trinity and predestination. He believed so strongly in one

35

Barton W. Stone

God that the idea of the Trinity disrupted even his prayer life. For a while he taught at a Methodist school in Georgia, but soon made a trek across Tennessee and Kentucky in 1796, preaching and searching for God's will for his life.

Stone eventually sought ordination from the Transylvania Presbytery at Cane Ridge, Kentucky, where he had been preaching for two years. He still had serious doubts about the doctrine of the Trinity found in the Westminster Confession of Faith (the basic creed of the Presbyterians). The church authorities required agreement with this confession for ordination. After some discussion with the presbytery, one of its members asked if he would adopt the Confession of Faith. He replied, "I do, as far as I see it consistent with the word of God." This reply was common among those trained in the revival tradition in Presbyterianism, and so satisfied the presbytery. Members ordained Stone and assigned him to minister to the churches at Cane Ridge and Concord, Kentucky, in 1798.

THE CANE RIDGE REVIVAL

In August 1801, Cane Ridge was the site of the largest and most well-known camp meeting in the nation's history. A wave of revivals led by James McGready and others had broken out in southern Kentucky in 1800. At the Cane Ridge revival, crowds estimated from 10,000 to 30,000 heard Baptist, Methodist, and Presbyterian ministers preach the gospel. During their preaching, many listeners experienced what Stone and others called "religious exercises." Some fell to the ground in a faint as if they were dead. Some jerked back and forth and made a sound like a dog's bark. Others felt the bodily agitations coming upon them and tried to run away. Some danced back and forth in place. A few laughed a hearty, solemn laugh.

How should today's Christians understand these experiences—falling, jerks, barks, running, dancing, laughing? All his life Barton Stone believed they were evidence of God's Spirit falling on those convicted of their sins at Cane Ridge. Does this make Stone a pentecostal or charismatic Christian? No. According to his autobiography, he believed that the exercises at Cane Ridge had been sparked by the circumstances of the times, including natural disasters and a heightened expectation of the nearness of the end of time. He never thought the exercises had to be the universal experience of all Christians. In other words, Stone believed God could use any circumstance to bring people to an experience of God. Though God's Spirit may work in dramatic ways in some cases, as at Cane Ridge, one can be a mature, faithful Christian without these unusual spiritual exercises.

Still, the Cane Ridge Revival had a profound effect on Stone and others. It convinced them of the importance of Christian unity. If God's Spirit appeared in response to Baptist, Methodist, and Presbyterian preaching, then the differences between these denominations must not be matters of the gospel. The unity among Christians produced by God should be a goal of all who claim to follow Christ. In Stone's words, "Let Christian unity be our polar star."

The experiences of Cane Ridge also increased the doubts that Stone and his fellow ministers had about Calvinistic predestination. They had seen many freely respond to God during the revivals.

The sanctuary that now shelters the Cane Ridge Meetinghouse

37

They felt more at home with a belief that human beings could respond to God's grace through their own limited but real free will.

THE LAST WILL AND TESTAMENT

This desire for unity soon proved itself in concrete action. The Presbyterian Synod of Kentucky questioned Stone and five other ministers about their support of the revival, their more open stance toward other Christians, and their doubts about Calvinism. Before the Synod could discipline them, they broke away and formed their own church association, the Springfield Presbytery. Within a year, they decided the Springfield Presbytery itself worked against biblical unity so they decided to disband it. They gave their reasons for doing so in *The Last Will and Testament of the Springfield Presbytery* written in 1804. This document is so significant in Stone-Campbell history that we provide it here in its entirety (including its nineteenth-century grammar and style):

> The PRESBYTERY OF SPRINGFIELD, sitting at Cane-ridge, in the county of Bourbon, being, through a gracious Providence, in more than ordinary bodily health, growing in strength and size daily; and in perfect soundness and composure of mind; but knowing that it is appointed for all delegated bodies once to die: and considering that the life of every such body is very uncertain, do make, and ordain this our Last Will and Testament, in manner and form following, viz.:
>
> *Imprimis.* We *will,* that this body die, be dissolved, and sink into union with the Body of Christ at large; for there is but one body, and one spirit, even as we are called in one hope of our calling.
>
> *Item.* We *will,* that our name of distinction, with its *Reverend* title, be forgotten, that there be but one Lord over God's heritage, and his name one.
>
> *Item.* We *will,* that our power of making laws for the government of the church, and executing them by delegated authority, forever cease; that the people may have free course to the Bible, and adopt *the law of the spirit of life in Christ Jesus.*

38

Item. We *will,* that candidates for the Gospel ministry henceforth study the Holy scriptures with fervent prayer, and obtain license from God to preach the simple Gospel, *with the Holy Ghost sent down from heaven,* without any mixture of philosophy, vain deceit, traditions of men, or the rudiments of the world. And let none henceforth take *this honor to himself, but he that is called of God, as was Aaron.*

Item. We *will,* that the church of Christ assume her native right of internal government--try her candidates for the ministry, as to their soundness in the faith, acquaintance with experimental religion, gravity and aptness to teach; and admit no other proof of their authority but Christ speaking in them. We will that the church of Christ look up to the Lord of the harvest to send forth labourers into his harvest; and that she resume her primitive right of trying those *who say they are Apostles, and are not.*

Item. We *will,* that each particular church, as a body, actuated by the same spirit, choose her own preacher, and support him by a free will offering, without written *call* or *subscription*--admit members--remove offences; and never henceforth *delegate* her right of government to any man or set of men whatever.

Item. We *will,* that the people henceforth take the Bible as the only sure guide to heaven; and as many as are offended with other books, which stand in competition with it, may cast them into the fire if they choose: for it is better to enter into life having one book, than having many to be cast into hell.

Item. We *will,* that preachers and people, cultivate a spirit of mutual forbearance; pray more and dispute less; and while they behold the signs of the times, look up, and confidently expect that redemption draweth nigh.

Item. We *will,* that our weak brethren, who may have been wishing to make the Presbytery of Springfield their king, and wot not what is now become of it, betake themselves to the Rock of Ages, and follow Jesus for the future.

Item. We *will,* that the Synod of Kentucky examine every member, who may be *suspected* of having departed from the Confession of Faith, and suspend every such suspected heretic immediately; in order that the oppressed may go free, and taste the sweets of gospel liberty.

Item. We will, that Ja---, the author of two letters lately published in Lexington, be encouraged in his zeal to destroy *partyism.* We will, moreover, that our past conduct be examined into by all who may have correct information; but let foreigners beware of speaking evil of things which they know not.

Item. Finally we *will,* that all our *sister bodies* read their Bibles carefully, that they may see their fate there determined, and prepare for death before it is too late.

Predestination ???

Signed by Stone and five other ministers, this document issued a clear call for restoration and unity. Much of it still remains influential for Disciples of Christ. The document reflected the cultural trend toward individual liberty in matters of religion, and echoed Thomas Jefferson's political emphasis on the sovereign will of the individual. The experience of these ministers at Cane Ridge had convinced them that all human beings could believe in God, if only they would listen to the gospel. God loved all persons, not just a select few who happened to be predestined to become Christian. This kind of theological development created an opening for women's leadership in the movement, though they struggled mightily to accomplish it. It also empowered ethnic groups, like African-Americans, who for decades would seek equality in Disciples church life, an equality that should naturally have accompanied a theological commitment that God loves all human beings.

The Last Will and Testament of the Springfield Presbytery expressed the desire of these ministers to develop congregations with the ability to choose their own ministers, without external interference. While their ministers would be ordained with certain authority and responsibility, they would not be rule-making "reverends." Their document emphasized that Christians should follow the Bible alone. A spirit of cooperation and freedom should prevail. Christians should "pray more and dispute less," and "confidently expect" that their redemption is on the horizon.

THE GROWTH OF THE STONE MOVEMENT

At the suggestion of Rice Haggard, a former associate of James O'Kelly, Stone and his followers soon called themselves "Christians" and established congregations they called Churches of Christ or Christian Churches. By 1807, the question of baptism arose in the movement. Eventually the Stone churches practiced believer's immersion but did not make it an absolute test of fellowship. Those baptized as infants could still be members and participate fully in the life of the church. Stone feared that making believer's immersion a test of fellowship would exclude more Christians than any creed.

Stone faced vehement opposition in response to two of his theological positions. He denied the substitutionary view of the atonement, the idea that Christ paid our debt to God on the cross. To Stone, such a view made God a hateful tyrant demanding payment instead of a loving parent offering grace. He also would not affirm the traditional doctrine of the Trinity, although he did describe Jesus as the "son of God." On these issues, Stone insisted on the literal wording of the Bible, accusing others of developing speculative theology.

Yet in spite of Stone's theological opponents, the defection of some of his co-laborers to the Shakers, and the return of others to the Presbyterians, by the 1820s the Stone Movement had grown to more than 10,000 members and spread from Kentucky and Ohio to Tennessee, Alabama, Missouri, and Illinois. A great deal of this growth resulted from whole congregations of Separate Baptists giving up their "Baptist" name to be "Christians."

This growth also emerged from the example and character of Barton W. Stone. His paper, *The Christian Messenger* (published 1826-1844), spread the message of his peaceful spirit and love for all far and wide. Although Stone continued to discuss his objections to substitutionary atonement and traditional Trinitarianism in his paper, he focused more often on the Christian themes of tolerance and unity. Soon he would make his unity teaching concrete by combining his movement with one led by Thomas and Alexander Campbell.

Thus by 1804 there were three independent movements in America attempting to be "Christians only." Although there were differences among them, having come from three different denominations—Methodists, Baptists, and Presbyterians—their similarities are striking. All three wanted the Bible alone to be their creed. All took the name "Christian." All organized themselves congregationally, without the control of a bishop or a clergy-led presbytery. Each worked to promote Christian unity. All sought to preach the gospel far and wide. These "restoration movements" were to have a lasting heritage in the United States.

FOR FURTHER READING:

Conkin, Paul K. *American Originals: Homemade Varieties of Christianity.* Chapel Hill: University of North Carolina Press, 1997. See pages 8-14.

Cummins, D. Duane. *The Disciples: A Struggle for Reformation.* St. Louis: Chalice Press, 2009. See pages 23-37.

Garrett, Leroy. *The Stone-Campbell Movement.* Joplin, Mo.: College Press, 1994. See pages 71-95.

North, James B. *Union in Truth: An Interpretive History of the Restoration Movement.* Cincinnati: Standard Publishing, 1994. See pages 33-70.

Webb, Henry E. *In Search of Christian Unity.* 1990; new edition, Abilene: Abilene Christian University Press, 2003. See pages 48-65.

West, Earl Irvin. *The Search for the Ancient Order,* Vol. 1. Nashville: Gospel Advocate, 1986. See pages 18-35.

Williams, D. Newell. *Barton Stone, A Spiritual Biography.* St Louis: Chalice Press, 2000.

QUESTIONS FOR DISCUSSION

1. List and discuss at least five themes found in *The Last Will and Testament of the Springfield Presbytery* that still influence Disciples of Christ. What else can we learn from this document?

2. Why do you think Stone objected to the idea of substitutionary atonement, that Jesus paid our debt of sin to alleviate God's anger toward us? What does this doctrine imply about God?

3. How important is the doctrine of the Trinity? How important has it been in your own experience of the Disciples of Christ?

4. What are the similarities and differences among the three "Christian" groups we have discussed so far (the Baptist, Methodist, and Presbyterian movements)?

THE COMING OF THE CAMPBELLS

While O'Kelly, Smith, Jones, and Stone were forming Christian groups in North America, Thomas Campbell (1763-1854) was still in Ireland. The religious pilgrimage of the Campbell family is interesting. Thomas's father, Archibald Campbell, was an Anglican converted from Roman Catholicism. Thomas converted to the Presbyterian Church of Scotland, becoming a minister for the Ahorey Church in Rich Hill, Ireland.

While in Ireland, Thomas Campbell became dissatisfied with the narrowness of his church, the Old Light, Anti-Burgher, Seceder Presbyterian Church. Each of these terms denoted a previous split among the Presbyterians. Campbell longed for the unity that the early church enjoyed and even made several unsuccessful attempts to unite the different factions in the Seceder Church in Ireland.

In 1807, Thomas came to the United States to escape the religious and political strife in Ireland, leaving his family behind to join him later. Assigned to preach in Western Pennsylvania, Campbell soon found himself in trouble for allowing Presbyterians of all stripes to take the Lord's Supper. Censured by his presbytery and synod, Campbell began an inter-denominational Bible study group, patterned on British missionary and Bible societies, known as the Christian Association of Washington, Pennsylvania. He refused to back down on his commitment to seek unity among Christians living in close proximity to one another on the frontier.

THE *DECLARATION AND ADDRESS*

In 1809, the Christian Association commissioned Thomas Campbell to write a document outlining the purpose of the organization and its plan for unity among Christians. This *Declaration and Address* (a reference to the freedom proclaimed by the American *Declaration of Independence*) made a clear call back to the freedom found in the New Testament as a basis for Christian unity.

One can get lost in the nineteenth-century language of the *Declaration and Address*, but its main points include:

Requires Cultural Conformity

1. *A fervent call to Christian unity.* "That the Church of Christ on earth is essentially, intentionally, and constitutionally one." It is one in essence because Christians are "subjects of the same grace, objects of the same divine love, bought with the same price, and joint heirs of the same inheritance." God intends the church to be one, evidenced by Jesus' fervent prayer for unity in John 17. The "constitution" that makes the church one is the New Testament.

Allows for Communal

2. *A strong condemnation of division among Christians.* "That division among Christians is a horrid evil, fraught with many evils." Thus, there should "be no schisms, no uncharitable divisions among them."

opinion becomes more important than Text. Interpretation according to who.

3. *Doctrinal differences not based on the express teachings of the New Testament are the causes of division.* More than sixty times in the *Declaration and Address*, Campbell uses phrases like "expressly exhibited," "plain," and "clear" to describe the binding teachings of scripture. Where the Bible is unclear or silent, no disagreement should divide Christians. Thomas Campbell never spelled out exactly what those "express teachings" are. Neither does he address the difficulty of Christians strongly disagreeing over what the Bible "expressly" teaches. This would be a significant problem later in the Campbell Movement.

4. *A simple confession of faith in Jesus, not agreement with an elaborate creed, is all that is necessary for*

46

admission to the church. Thus, creeds, even if true and helpful, should not be used to exclude Christians who disagree with them from full acceptance as children of God.

[handwritten margin note: Just opposed to creeds.]

5. *A desire to return to the purity of the first century church.* By removing items that have divided Christians and obscured the beauty of the church, God's people can experience personal and corporate holiness and purity.

[handwritten margin note: assumed Unity!]

6. *An appeal for love and understanding among Christians.* Those who confess faith in Christ "should consider each other as the precious saints of God, should love each other as brethren, children of the same family and Father, temples of the same Spirit, members of the same body . . . ."

[handwritten margin note: Believe]

Thomas Campbell never intended the principles of the *Declaration and Address* to be the basis of a new religious group. Instead, he hoped to issue a call to unity among Christians of all denominations. "The cause that we advocate is not our own peculiar cause, nor the cause of any party, considered as such; it is a common cause, the cause of Christ and our brethren of all denominations."

Thomas Campbell

Things changed when the Christian Association of Washington eventually formed the nucleus of a new congregation, the Brush Run Church. By forming a church, Campbell made his quest for Christian unity more difficult. Even today, in a Bible study group with people from different denominations, it seems as if we have much in common. Why can't we unite? But if that Bible study group were to become a church, then it would have to make certain decisions that would highlight the differences among its members. How will they worship? Who will lead them? Who can be a part of this church? What does the church

47

believe and teach? It is easier to talk about unity than to actually achieve it.

Having said this, we don't want to diminish the power of Thomas Campbell's call to Christian unity. The *Declaration and Address* reminds contemporary Disciples that if they are to be a biblical people they must continue to take Christ's prayer for unity seriously.

ALEXANDER CAMPBELL IN SCOTLAND

Mr ROBERT SANDEMAN.
Author of Letters on Theron and Aspasio
Views on Baptism &c.

Robert Sandeman

The rest of Thomas Campbell's family, including his oldest son Alexander (1788-1866), soon boarded a ship from Ireland to join him in Pennsylvania. Storms shipwrecked the ship off the coast of Scotland. Consequently, the family spent close to a year in Glasgow (1808-1809), allowing Alexander to attend classes at the university there.

While in Glasgow, Alexander made friends with Greville Ewing and others who had broken from the Church of Scotland and formed independent churches. Ewing was associated with two brothers, James and Robert Haldane, who in turn were influenced by the thought of John Glas and Robert Sandeman. Glas, Sandeman, the Haldanes, and Ewing all wished to return to the practices of the New Testament church. Although they did not agree on every detail, these practices included local church leadership by elders, weekly Lord's Supper, love feasts with footwashing and the holy kiss, believer's baptism by immersion, opposition to ministerial titles such as "Reverend," and separation of church and state. During his stay in Glasgow, Alexander never joined any of these independent churches, but he became increasingly dissatisfied with what he perceived as the narrowness of the Seceder Presbyterians.

FATHER AND SON REUNION

After landing in New York, the family reunited in Western Pennsylvania in October 1809. Both Thomas and Alexander told of their separate difficulties with the Seceder Presbyterian Church. Alexander read a proof copy of the *Declaration and Address* and pledged to devote his life to promoting the principles he found there. Alexander began to study for the ministry under his father, and when the Brush Run Church began in 1811, both father and son did their share of the preaching.

Alexander Campbell

In 1811, Alexander married Margaret Brown, the daughter of a farmer who lived just over the line in what is now West Virginia. They lived on her father's farm until he eventually deeded the property to them. This property, in what came to be known as Bethany, West Virginia, became the home of Alexander Campbell and the center of the movement he led until his death.

A year after their marriage, Margaret and Alexander had their first child, Jane. Though bringing with it a time of celebration and joy, the birth of Jane also presented the family with its own theological crisis. Some in the Brush Run Church had questioned the validity of their infant baptism and requested immersion as adults. Thus, Alexander Campbell faced a decision. Should he baptize his infant daughter? Should he himself be baptized? After months of study, he concluded that the immersion of believers, not the sprinkling of infants, represented the biblical model of baptism. In June 1812, Matthias Luce, a Baptist minister, baptized Alexander and Thomas Campbell along with their wives and three others from the Brush Run Church.

Soon most members at Brush Run were immersed as believers. On the one hand, these acts of baptism further separated the Campbells from their Presbyterian roots, since Presbyterians believed they should baptize infants for several reasons, particularly to cleanse them from their participation in the sin they inherited from Adam. On the other hand, the practice of believer's immersion brought the Campbells into the orbit of the Baptists on the frontier. After much discussion, the Brush Run Church joined the Redstone Baptist Association in 1815.

REFORMERS AMONG THE BAPTISTS

Joining the Redstone Baptist Association might look like an abandonment of the Campbells' goal to unite all Christians. How could they call for Christian unity when they belonged to a particular denomination? The Campbells, however, especially Thomas, did not see things that way. Any step toward visible unity became a step toward the ultimate unity of Christians. Becoming part of a Baptist Association was preferable to existing solely as an individual congregation.

For the next fifteen years, Thomas and Alexander Campbell worked as reformers among the Baptists. New congregations associated with the Campbells began to dot the countryside. Alexander Campbell became influential through his work as an educator, publisher, and debater. From 1818-1823 he educated young people for the ministry in his home. In 1823, he began a monthly periodical, the *Christian Baptist*. The tone of the paper was iconoclastic, attacking traditional institutions, particularly the power of the clergy. Alexander was determined to tear down every practice that stood in the way of restoring New Testament Christianity and the unity of the early church.

Although teaching and writing gave him some notoriety, his debating made Alexander Campbell a household name on the frontier. In the beginning, the Campbells had opposed disputes and debates as antithetical to Christian unity. But religious and political debating was a common practice. After the Baptists approached him several times to defend believer's immersion in debate, Alexander finally agreed. In 1820, he faced John Walker and in 1823, William Maccalla, each Presbyterian ministers who argued for infant baptism. These debates, especially in their printed forms, were widely influential and convinced even Thomas Campbell that debating could be a positive way to advance the cause of restoration and unity.

Although his debates made him the champion of believer's immersion, other teachings made Alexander suspect among many of the Baptists. As early as 1816, he offended many Baptists with his "Sermon on the Law" delivered at the meeting of the Redstone Association. In the sermon, Campbell made a sharp distinction between the Old and New Testaments, arguing that the Law of

Moses was not authoritative for determining the beliefs and actions of the church. This upset Baptist preachers who used the Old Testament to justify many of their practices.

Strong opposition from certain ministers in the Redstone Association led Campbell to transfer his membership to a congregation in the Mahoning Baptist Association, a group more favorable to Campbell's reforms. The churches of the Mahoning Association grew significantly due to the evangelism of Walter Scott (see Chapter Six). Jealousy of that growth and the increasing realization that the Campbells did not accept Baptist beliefs concerning such things as the meaning of baptism and the role of the minister soon caused other Baptist Associations to turn against them. Eventually some associations excluded Baptist churches that supported Campbell. Consequently, the Mahoning Association dissolved itself in 1830, and numerous Baptist Associations throughout Virginia, Ohio, and adjacent states also dissolved or divided. The Disciples emerged as a distinct group to build its own style of cooperation to fulfill the mission of the church beyond local congregations.

RACE AND THE EARLY DISCIPLES

By the time of the breakup of the Mahoning Association in 1830, there were more than two million enslaved African Americans in the United States (in a total population of just under thirteen million, meaning more than 15% of the population). Increasingly, as the Campbell Movement emerged from the Baptists, Christians were expected to indicate where they stood on this practice (see Chapter Eight). Among the growing Disciples churches, a small minority were abolitionists, people like John Boggs and his *North-Western Christian Magazine*, and Ovid Butler at Northwestern University in Indianapolis. There were also strong advocates for slavery, located mostly in the southern part of the country, represented by Disciples leader James Shannon, president of Bacon College in Kentucky (1840-1850), who later became president of the University of Missouri (1850-1856).

A number of Disciples, including most of the founders, took a position toward the middle of the debate. Most hoped for gradual emancipation, arguing that society needed to make appropriate preparations for freedom, in educating blacks and changing the hearts of whites. For awhile, Barton Stone participated in the American Colonization Society that purchased, educated, and then sent blacks to Africa. In 1845, Alexander Campbell published a series of articles that, essentially, put forward a biblical defense of slavery. Yet, he also argued that, in the United States, the practice had become disgraceful and indefensible. Campbell made the unity of Christians, North and South, his "grandest object," which meant he feared that addressing this divisive issue would destroy the growing movement. As has often happened in the history of the Disciples, a concern to maintain unity at all cost translated into an avoidance of efforts to connect the gospel message clearly to the need to right a grave social injustice. While Alexander Campbell hoped for the eventual freedom of enslaved persons, he worked harder to avoid the controversy than to do anything meaningfully to contribute to emancipation. In fact, Disciples in the developing South enslaved significant numbers of African Americans.

By 1820, African Americans had joined congregations related to the Stone-Campbell Movement. Records of the two earliest congregations, those of Cane Ridge (Barton Stone) in Kentucky and Brush Run in Pennsylvania, list African Americans as members. By 1852, Cane Ridge had listed 124 members, seventy-one of whom were black. A few became early preachers in the movement. Two black preachers, Samuel Buckner and Alexander Campbell were ordained by Disciples to preach and establish churches in the southern states of North Carolina and Kentucky. Early in Disciples history, mixed-race congregations were the norm. In white-controlled congregations, black leadership experienced serious limitations. A few congregations contained African American "exhorters" and deacons, who preached only to black members and performed the tasks of pastoral care to minister to their needs. One could easily argue that black leaders were appointed to perform these tasks mostly because white leaders, deeply infected with racial bias, viewed pastoral care for black members as beneath them.

Both Thomas Campbell and Alexander Campbell viewed evangelization among African Americans as an important task. The elder Campbell, for example, taught black children in Kentucky in 1819. The younger Campbell routinely preached among African

Americans and connected them to white congregations developing in Western Virginia, Ohio, and Pennsylvania. Though prejudice and racism remained part of the experience in the churches, blacks were drawn to the Disciples message because of its accessibility to all. One did not have to wait to be "elected" by God, but rather could simply accept the love God offered freely to all. Black membership in white-controlled churches constituted full membership, though African Americans were often relegated to the rear of the congregation or to balconies or basements. They suffered numerous other indignities, including being the last to receive the Lord's Supper and being excluded from most aspects of congregational governance.

By the late 1830s, numbers of autonomous African American congregations developed. The earliest most likely appeared in Midway, Kentucky in 1834, with the black Alexander Campbell as its pastor. Another appeared in Pickerelltown, Ohio in 1838, with Henry Newson as pastor, who led the congregation to serve as a stop on the Underground Railroad for a time. Peter Lowery, a black Nashville preacher, provided early leadership for African Americans after buying his own freedom in 1840, freeing his family by 1846, and forming a mixed congregation that eventually reached more than 500 members. By 1861, there were at least 7,000 black members among Disciples. In 1867, Lowery founded the Tennessee Manual Labor University, the first organized educational effort among Disciples for African American higher education.

DISCIPLES OF CHRIST

After their break with the Baptists, Campbell's churches faced the question of what to call themselves. Many individual followers preferred the name "Christian." Congregations often called themselves by a community name, "the Brush Run Church" or the "Wellsburg Church." Sometimes a sign on the outside of the building read, "Church of Christ" or "Christian Church."

This confusion of names was in many ways intentional. They did not want an exclusive sectarian or denominational name. They wanted to call all Christians to unity. Nevertheless, one name increasingly characterized this congregationally organized church—Disciples of Christ. Alexander Campbell particularly preferred this name to "Christian." After all, the followers of Jesus were called Disciples before they were called Christians. He also did not want the congregations of his movement to be confused with those of the Christian movements (see Chapter Two) of New England and Virginia or even the one led by Barton Stone.

Yet, the similarities between these Disciples and the Stone Christians were so obvious that the two groups would eventually unite, although without the strong support of Alexander Campbell. The next chapter tells that part of the story.

FOR FURTHER READING

Conkin, Paul K. *American Originals: Homemade Varieties of Christianity.* Chapel Hill: University of North Carolina Press, 1997. See pages 14-22.

Cummins, D. Duane. *The Disciples: A Struggle for Reformation.* St. Louis: Chalice Press, 2009. See pages 38-66.

Garrett, Leroy. *The Stone-Campbell Movement.* Joplin, Mo.: College Press, 1994. See pages 97-141.

Hughes, Richard T. *Reviving the Ancient Faith: The Story of Churches of Christ in America.* 1996; new edition, Abilene: Abilene Christian University Press, 2008. See pages 21-135.

Olbricht, Thomas H. and Hans Rollmann. *The Quest for Christian Unity, Peace, and Purity in Thomas Campbell's Declaration and Address.* Lanham, Md.: Scarecrow Press, 2000.

Webb, Henry E. *In Search of Christian Unity.* 1990; new edition, Abilene: Abilene Christian University Press, 2003. See pages 67-129.

QUESTIONS FOR DISCUSSION

1. Briefly describe Thomas Campbell's plan for producing Christian unity. What parts of that plan seem least workable? What parts seem appropriate today?

2. What are the ways Alexander Campbell spread his ideas among the Baptists?

3. As Campbell's movement dissolved its affiliation with the Baptists, it began to emerge as a "church" or "denomination" in its own right. What were the implications of this move for Disciples?

4. How did the church leaders he met in Scotland affect the ideas Alexander Campbell later had about the church?

5. How did cultural prejudices relating to race affect the ability of Disciples to be faithful to their understanding of the gospel?

6. Why did Alexander Campbell prefer the name "Disciples"?

THE STONE AND CAMPBELL MOVEMENTS UNITE

Take a map of the United States in 1820 and begin drawing concentric circles around the Stone Movement's strongholds. Do the same for the Campbell Movement, and you will see the circles begin to intersect in western Virginia, Ohio, and Kentucky. Especially in these last two states, members of the two groups were increasingly in close contact with one another. In many towns, like Georgetown and Lexington, Kentucky, there were congregations associated with each group.

Alexander Campbell first visited Kentucky in 1823, and the next year he met Stone in the living room of Stone's Georgetown home. The two sensed a close kinship of ideas and goals and expressed great respect for one another. Later in life, Stone said there were fewer faults in Campbell than in any man he knew, acknowledging that Campbell was the greatest promoter of the religious reformation in which they both were involved. In Stone's obituary notice in the 1844 *Millennial Harbinger,* Campbell hailed Stone as the instrument of bringing many out of human tradition to accept the message of the Bible as their confession of faith and rule of life.

COMPARING THE MEN AND THEIR MOVEMENTS

Campbell and Stone always regarded each other with a bit of uneasiness. Certainly there were educational and economic differences between them. Campbell was a wealthy farmer and landowner

57

while Stone often lived near the edge of poverty. Campbell had studied at the University of Glasgow while Stone possessed on-the-job training and went to school at a frontier academy. They were different personalities in many ways. Something else, however, gave an edge to their relationship.

Stone believed the purpose of this religious reformation was to create lives characterized by the spirit of Christ. The love, humility, patience, and joy described as the fruit of the Spirit were the ultimate goals—the real tests of success. Stone sought to nurture these foundational traits by freeing people from the shackles of creeds and denominational structures to rely on the Bible alone. Only when believers embodied those virtues could Christians unite and bring reform. He regarded Alexander Campbell as too rigid on certain doctrines resulting in a de-emphasis on the work of God's Spirit.

Campbell, in contrast, thought that Stone and the other "Christian" groups were too lax in their theological reflection. The New England Christians especially were quite unorthodox in their thinking about God and the work of Christ. Most rejected Trinitarian theology and some taught universalism—that God would eventually save all people. Campbell's platform for reform stressed a return to the ancient gospel—the beliefs and practices of the early church. He certainly believed that true submission to Christ would result in the fruit of the Spirit so important to Stone. But Campbell believed restoring the doctrinal details seen in the New Testament would reform the church and bring Christian unity.

Campbell and Stone still shared much in common. They were committed to the scriptures as the true source of light, life, and authority. They were committed to ending the shameful divisions among followers of Christ, and therefore opposed anything that separated Christians including creeds, clergy, unscriptural names, and denominational structures. They believed that the church depicted in the New Testament was the ideal church, pure and free from all the corruptions of the ages. They hoped to restore that church in their own time.

Early Moves toward Union and Difficulties

As early as the 1820s, members of the two bodies began asking why they weren't one. In August 1831, Stone replied to the question in his paper the *Christian Messenger*. He saw no reason they should not visibly unite since they were already one in spirit. Any reluctance to unite came from the Reformers—the Campbell people—not from those affiliated with him. He saw two reasons for their hesitance. First, the Stone Movement allowed unimmersed people to be members of their churches and to take communion. Stone churches taught that people were to believe, repent, and be immersed for the forgiveness of sins. But they did not make immersion as crucial to Christianity as the Campbell Movement had. They taught the importance of immersion, but fully accepted those who were not convinced.

The second thing keeping them apart was the name each group had chosen. Like the Smith-Jones and O'Kelly churches, the Stone Movement had always simply used the name Christian. Campbell preferred the label Disciples, which Stone accepted as a good scriptural name. But the Campbell churches used it, Stone asserted, to make sure no one confused them with the groups called Christian. He described Disciples as a party name, just like Presbyterian or Baptist, because it distinguished those churches from other bodies of believers. Campbell responded with a sharp rebuke, claiming no one expected them to give up the scriptural name Christian.

These articles and others that followed mirrored the deep differences between the two men and their movements. First, Barton Stone opposed traditional understandings of the Trinity. He did not believe the New Testament taught the Trinity, but that it had appeared in human creeds and confessions, especially the Westminster Confession. His rejection of the Trinity also, of course, affected his view of Jesus. He accepted every biblical statement about Christ at face value without question. But for him that meant accepting that Christ and God could not be equal or the same. Christ was Son of God and Savior; God exalted Christ to a place above all others and seated Christ at God's right hand; but Christ was not equal to God. The equality of God and Christ simply didn't make sense to Stone.

Campbell, in contrast, was quite traditional in his views of God and the nature of Christ. While he agreed that the word "Trinity" was not in the Bible, he believed the sense of the community within God—one deity yet three persons—was essential to the Christian faith. For Campbell, to demote Christ from full

59

divinity questioned the very center of Christian belief, that Jesus is able to save human beings.

Despite his strong rejection of Calvinist predestination, Stone held a rather pessimistic view of human nature. Humans were capable of understanding and responding appropriately to the gospel message. Yet he saw a wide role for the Holy Spirit as necessary in convicting and converting sinners. Stone believed that human history was itself stuck in a downward spiral which only the second coming of Christ could stop.

Campbell saw things very differently. He had an optimistic view of human beings, believing they could change everything by using their heads and working hard. God had prepared the United States for the restoration of the church through "the ancient gospel and order of things." After this restoration, all true Christians would come together, convert the world, and bring in the thousand-year reign of peace and prosperity on earth.

Stone and Campbell also differed in their approach to evangelism. Stone had been a proponent of the revivals since his own experience at Cane Ridge. He believed the Holy Spirit worked on the hearts of people to convict and convert them. Campbell disliked the revivals and their raucous approach to conversion. Calm, clear, rational teaching of the gospel spelled out in the New Testament would convey truth and convince people to respond. The Holy Spirit worked through and alongside the written word, never separately from it, to convince and convert sinners to Jesus.

These two Christian leaders also differed in their beliefs about baptism. Campbell certainly believed there were those who enjoyed the benefits of Christ's pardon and salvation who had never been immersed because of innocent misunderstanding. He did teach, however, that in order to be part of the reform—to be a member in one of the churches in his movement—a person must be immersed. While Stone and his followers taught immersion, they practiced "open membership," allowing non-immersed believers to be full members who could participate fully in the life of their churches.

The two movements also differed in their views of both the Lord's Supper and the ministry. The Stone churches celebrated the Lord's Supper infrequently while the Campbell churches celebrated it every week. The Stone churches had a much more developed sense of the ministry. They distinguished between elders who were ordained ministers and those who were not officially ordained. The Campbell churches were extremely anti-clergy and much more democratic in their attitudes about who could do what in the church.

These were not minor differences! They reflected contradictory understandings of the nature of God, humankind, salvation, the church, and the end of time. How could two movements as dissimilar as these even consider uniting? It is hard to imagine, but thousands in both movements were convinced that the things they held in common far outweighed their differences. They agreed on the rejection of human creeds and confessions as tests of fellowship. They rejected loyalty to denominational bodies that separated them from other believers. All had a commitment to God and shared a belief in the trustworthiness of the Bible. All sought the unity of Christ's church.

Still, there were practical matters that made union a difficult undertaking. Neither group had central offices to make pronouncements about a union. Each local congregation possessed the only governing authority in either movement. There were no edicts from on high—the union had to happen in each city, town, or village throughout the country. There had been stirrings of union as early as 1828 between a Stone congregation and a Campbell congregation in Bourbon County, Kentucky. A union did take place in Millersburg, Kentucky, in April 1831 and shortly afterward in Georgetown. However, meetings on December 31, 1831, and January 1, 1832, in Lexington, Kentucky, provided the real spark for the union between the two groups.

THE UNION TAKES SHAPE

Barton Stone, then living in Georgetown, had become fast friends with John T. Johnson (1788-1856), a former Baptist preacher who now followed Alexander Campbell's reform ideas. They had persuaded the two congregations in Georgetown to unite and proposed to hold four-day conferences at Georgetown on Christmas weekend and at the Hill Street church in Lexington on New Year's weekend to discuss the union efforts. In Lexington, over two or three days, several leaders from the two groups spoke, including one of the most widely known leaders of the Campbell movement in Kentucky, Raccoon John Smith (1784-1868). Some of the speakers did not

John Smith   John Rogers

believe it wise to try for a quick union between the two groups. They favored a gradual process that would allow them to grow together more naturally.

But the union occurred more quickly than some advised. Stone and Smith were the final speakers at the concluding session Saturday afternoon. Stone asked Smith to go first. Smith spoke of the fact that God has only one people on earth and that the Bible, the one book God had given Christians, exhorts them to be one family. He openly admitted that there were serious differences between the two groups, mentioning the issues of God's nature, the Trinity, and the atonement. These have been topics of discussion for centuries, he exclaimed, and are as far from settled now as they ever have been. The precise positions that Christians might take on these or any number of other issues are not part of the gospel. God did not promise heaven to those who hold one position or the other, nor did God threaten hell to those who deny them.

Only two things kept them from uniting immediately, Smith continued. Both groups should stop making deductions and inferences from scripture into requirements for fellowship, but should simply use the words of scripture when they spoke about these things. There should be more love for one another. Then Smith made one of the most famous statements in Stone-Campbell history: "Let us then, my brethren, be no longer Campbellites or Stoneites, New Lights or Old Lights, or any other kind of lights.

But let us come to the Bible and the Bible alone, as the only book in creation that can give us all the Light we need."

Stone, after a brief statement, concluded that he had no objection to the basis of union Smith had laid down. He then turned and gave Smith his hand in fellowship, symbolizing their new unity. The next day, Sunday, January 1, 1832, the two congregations met together and took the Lord's Supper as one body. This service seemed to seal the union.

Elated, Stone delivered a report of the meeting in the *Christian Messenger*. He described the spirit of union as spreading like fire in dry stubble. The elders and people together had commissioned John Smith and John Rogers (1800-1867), formerly of the Campbell and Stone movements respectively, to travel among the churches to tell them what had happened in Lexington in order to "increase and consolidate the union." Smith and Rogers spent three years doing just that. Campbell took notice of the meeting in the March issue of his *Millennial Harbinger*, concluding that if the groups present really had renounced their speculations, there was nothing to do but bid them Godspeed.

FURTHER ROADBLOCKS TO UNION

The road to unity did not come easily, however. For many on both sides, the union seemed to mean giving up things they held dear. The old tensions over worship style were still there—the Stone congregations being more expressive, the Campbell churches more rational and dignified. Notions about the work of the Holy Spirit and the name of the church continued to be problems for some. The Smith-Jones and O'Kelly Christian Churches that had been in fellowship with the Stone Movement were shocked at the union. They regarded Alexander Campbell as cold and rationalistic and suspected he had little or no real religion in him. They charged Stone with giving up the original vision of their reform.

A number of Stone congregations that chose not to participate in the union shared that sentiment. Most remained part of the loosely connected body of Christian Churches that included the churches of the Smith-Jones and O'Kelly Movements. As mentioned in Chapter Two, those churches merged in 1931 with the Congregational Church to form the Congregational Christian

Church. Finally, that body merged in 1957 with the Evangelical and Reformed Church to form what today is the United Church of Christ.

When Stone moved to Jacksonville, Illinois, in 1834, he found that the two congregations in the town, one associated with his movement and one with the Campbell movement, still worshipped separately. He refused to worship with either until they united. But the unity between the two movements continually proved difficult. Within weeks after the wonderful unity communion service on January 1, 1832, in Lexington, the two groups experienced what one reporter described as a "blow up." The Stone people insisted that there had to be an ordained minister (elder) present to administer the Lord's Supper. Since the Campbell people thought such a requirement ridiculous, the two groups in Lexington decided that they could not unite immediately. It took almost three more years before the two congregations actually accomplished their unity.

REAL UNITY

Even with all the problems involved, the story of the union of the Stone and Campbell Movements is a significant one. What made it possible for these two very different groups to come together? It happened because the people involved believed God wanted the union of their churches. They also affirmed that Christians are members of one body, one Spirit, one God, one faith, and one baptism. Most of all, they understood that they could love one another as fellow children of God, in spite of all their imperfections.

Christian unity may not always mean a physical merger of congregations or movements. But when Christians are convinced of the importance of unity and are willing to put up with each others' peculiarities in the knowledge that all are committed to exploring the full meaning of faith together, the kind of unity illustrated in this chapter can be discovered by others.

FOR FURTHER READING

Burnley, Lawrence A. Q. *The Cost of Unity: African-American Agency and Education in the Christian Church, 1865-1914.* Macon, Ga.: Mercer University Press, 2009.

Cummins, D. Duane. *The Disciples: A Struggle for Reformation.* St. Louis: Chalice Press, 2009. See pages 67-79.

Garrett, Leroy. *The Stone-Campbell Movement: The Story of the American Restoration Movement.* Joplin, Mo.: College Press, 1994. See pages 174-196.

Toulouse, Mark G. *Joined in Discipleship: The Shaping of Contemporary Disciples Identity.* St. Louis: Chalice Press, 1997. See pages 73-100.

Williams, John Augustus. *Life of Elder John Smith: With Some Account of the Rise and Progress of the Current Reformation.* Cincinnati: R. W. Carroll, 1871. See pages 367-378.

Williams, D. Newell. *Barton Stone: A Spiritual Biography.* St Louis: Chalice Press, 2000. See pages 183-194.

QUESTIONS FOR DISCUSSION

1. How did the personalities of Stone and Campbell help or hurt the union between their movements?

2. This union illustrates how unity can occur even when people do not agree on most theological issues. How important is it for members of local congregations within Disciples to agree on most theological issues?

3. What do you think was the most serious difference in belief between the Stone and Campbell Movements at the time of the union? Why do you think that one is the most serious?

4. Would the difference(s) in belief you chose in question three prevent you from approving a union with a group that held a view other than your own?

5. Would it be possible today for local congregations to experience a union like those that occurred in the 1830s and following? If so, how? If not, why not?

6. Is union an "essential" part of the church's identity? In other words, is the Christian church, by its very nature, a unified church, from God's point of view, that has not yet recognized the fact?

THE GROWTH OF THE STONE-CAMPBELL MOVEMENT

W hen the congregations associated with Stone and Campbell began to unite in 1832, their members numbered around 25,000, mainly living in Kentucky and Ohio. By 1861, the resulting movement numbered almost 200,000 in twenty-nine states and two territories. During this period, the Disciples of Christ (as they were generally known) became a nationwide church, by some estimates the fourth largest religious group in the country.

WALTER SCOTT AND THE NEW EVANGELISM

This phenomenal growth began with the intentional efforts of Walter Scott (1796-1861). Born in Scotland, Scott grew up in the Church of Scotland and received his education at the University of Edinburgh. In 1818, he came to the United States, eventually settling near Pittsburgh. There he taught school and worshipped with a Scottish Baptist church.

In 1821, Scott met Alexander Campbell, and they soon became friends. Scott contributed articles on evangelism to the initial issue of Campbell's *Christian Baptist* (Scott was the one who suggested the name for the journal). Campbell thought so highly of Scott that he nominated him for appointment as a traveling evangelist for the Mahoning Baptist Association.

In 1827, members of the Mahoning Association appointed Scott as their evangelist. The year before, the seventeen churches in the Association had a total of thirty-four baptisms. In his first

Walter Scott

year as evangelist, Scott had nearly a thousand baptisms, doubling the size of most of the churches. Indeed, by some counts Scott averaged a thousand baptisms per year for the next thirty years of his life.

Most have attributed Scott's success to the new method of evangelism he developed during this period. Although the churches of the Campbell Movement had been in existence for several years and all practiced believer's immersion, they had not formulated a simple answer to the question, "What must I do to be saved?" In his study of scripture, Scott found an answer which he described as "the ancient gospel" or (in the words of one of his later book titles) *The Gospel Restored.*

Scott originally summarized that gospel under six points. Humans should do three things to be saved: believe, repent, and be baptized. God makes three promises to those who do these things: forgiveness of sins, the gift of the Holy Spirit, and eternal life. Eventually, Scott reduced the six to five—faith, repentance, baptism, forgiveness of sins, and the gift of the Holy Spirit—a list he liked to tick off on the fingers of one hand, hence the formula came to be known as "the five-finger exercise."

Such a formula could easily become legalistic. Scott sought to avoid legalistic thinking by consistently emphasizing what he understood to be the central teaching of Christianity, that Jesus is the Christ. Scott called this "the golden oracle," later writing a massive volume entitled *The Messiahship, or Great Demonstration, Written for the Union of Christians, on Christian Principles, as Plead for in the Current Reformation.* This lengthy title shows that Scott's view of restoration was directly in line with that of Stone and the Campbells. Restoration centered on Christ for the purpose of uniting all Christians.

Why was Scott's "five-finger" approach so successful? Because many on the frontier were under the influence of a strict Calvinism that said one could do nothing to be saved, since salvation depended solely on the work of God's predestination. Many went to Calvinistic revivals and sat on the mourner's or anxious bench, trying to "pray through" until God sent a sign of their election. Many never received such a sign and felt rejected by God.

By contrast, Scott told these independent frontier people that there was something they could do to be saved. Salvation was for all those who would believe, repent, and be baptized. This placed salvation directly in their own hands. Many received this message with great relief and joy, rushing forward to confess their faith and be baptized.

Although Scott began his preaching of the restored gospel before the union with the Stone Movement in 1832, evangelists in the united movement copied his method, accounting for much of the growth of the Disciples through the nineteenth century. This is why many consider him one of the four founders of the movement along with Barton Stone, Thomas Campbell, and Alexander Campbell.

In truth, Walter Scott embodied the culture of his age. He reflected well the interest of most of the nineteenth-century evangelicals who sought to tame the morality of the frontier. In one essay in 1832, he lamented, "drinking and cursing are crying sins in Ohio." The modern reader in Ohio might long for the day that drinking and cursing were the major sins confronting the state! This approach to sin often meant that more attention was paid to matters of personal morality than the more systemic sins of the day, like slavery for example. While he believed in the importance of empowering women through education, he believed women ultimately belonged in the home taking care of hearth, children, and husband. More so than either Campbell or Stone, Walter Scott captured, both in person and in ministry, many of the contemporary cultural themes surrounding him.

Thus, in addition to noting his brief and simple expression of the "ancient gospel," one might also note that at least part of his evangelistic success most likely had some connection to his tremendous ability to articulate frontier themes so well, and with such oratorical flair. He also connected the "ancient gospel" to rousing singing. This found favor with frontier audiences as well. In 1839, Scott produced a hymnbook of more than 700 hymns, hoping to put a stop to "the endlessly repeated singing of the same hymn to the same tune, at present so common in our assemblies."

SCHOOLS AND COLLEGES

Many of the early leaders, including Thomas and Alexander Campbell, were teachers. It is not surprising, then, that the Stone-Campbell Movement, along with every major religious group in the nineteenth century, began colleges and schools. Unlike many other religious schools of the period, these colleges did not seek to educate ministers as their primary purpose. Instead, they focused on broad training in the arts and sciences using the empirical method popularized in seventeenth-century England and Scotland.

Bacon College, in Georgetown, Kentucky, founded in 1836 primarily as an engineering school, became the first Disciples college. Walter Scott served briefly as its president. Named after Sir Francis Bacon (1561-1626), the school emphasized his experimental method in the sciences and even in moral teaching. In 1839, Bacon College moved to Harrodsburg, Kentucky, was rechartered in 1858 as Kentucky University, and later merged with other schools to become Transylvania University in Lexington.

In 1841, Alexander Campbell founded Bethany College near his home in Bethany, West Virginia. Bethany also depended heavily on the empirical method, with more than half of the curriculum in the sciences. Bethany's charter prohibited the establishment of a theological professorship. At the same time, Campbell meant Bethany to be a college founded on the Bible. Students at Bethany heard a one-hour Bible lecture each day. This practice reflected the Disciples early disdain for the word theology and their insistence

Bethany College

on objective, empirical Bible study. Bethany College is still in its original location and remains one of the colleges associated with Disciples of Christ.

Franklin College near Nashville, Tennessee, began in 1845. Tolbert Fanning (1810-1874), the founder of the school, did not believe in endowments for colleges. That partially explains the short life of Franklin College. Closed by the Civil War in 1861, it reopened briefly in 1865, but soon closed permanently as the result of a campus fire.

For a while, these were the three major colleges for Disciples, although numerous schools and colleges sprang up wherever the movement spread. From 1840-1866, Disciples began thirty-two colleges including (with their founding dates) Burritt College, Spencer, Tennessee (1848); Hiram College, Hiram, Ohio (1850); Butler University, Indianapolis, Indiana (1854); Culver-Stockton College, Canton, Missouri (1853); and Eureka College, Eureka, Illinois (1855).

Although not intended primarily for ministerial education, the colleges served that function. Many of the significant leaders in the church in the nineteenth century were products of the colleges, particularly Bethany. In a congregationally organized movement, the colleges provided one means of fellowship and unity of thought among the churches.

PAPERS, PUBLICATIONS, AND DEBATES

Religious papers also provided unity (and sometimes disunity) for Disciples, serving as the forum to discuss ideas and issues. An old truism is that the Disciples did not have bishops but had editors who sometimes ruled with an iron fist.

Alexander Campbell's influence grew primarily through his monthly periodicals, first the *Christian Baptist* (1823-1830), then the *Millennial Harbinger* (1830-1866). There is a marked difference in tone between the two journals reflecting Campbell's changed circumstances. He filled the *Christian Baptist* with sarcastic denunciations of the religious follies of the age. The *Harbinger* exhibited a more positive tone, more appropriate considering Campbell's position as the leader of an emerging popular Christian movement among Protestants.

71

Other leaders greatly extended their influence through journals. Barton Stone edited the *Christian Messenger* from 1826-1844. Walter Scott had the aptly named *Evangelist* (1832-1844), and then the *Protestant Unionist* (1844-1848). In 1855, Tolbert Fanning (1810-1874) founded the influential *Gospel Advocate*. The *American Christian Review*, edited from 1858 by Benjamin Franklin (1812-1878), eventually became the most widely read paper among Disciples.

In addition, there were dozens of short-lived papers with limited circulation (including one named the *Heretic Detector*). These papers did indeed detect heresy, debate issues, promote unity, create disunity, and suggest programs. More than any other factor, the journals ultimately formed the web that kept the Stone-Campbell Movement together, in spite of their occasional attitude of "over-againstness" in relation to one another.

Other printed material besides periodicals helped shape Disciples thought, especially the published works of Alexander Campbell. Campbell published one of the first modern translations of the New Testament (usually known as the *Living Oracles*) in 1826, though the translation never became popular even among the Disciples. More influential was his *Christian System* (1836), the earliest systematic theology for Disciples (although Campbell would not have liked that description).

Religious debates were a common way of disseminating ideas in the nineteenth century. Campbell and his opponents debated with class, always in a respectful fashion, and drew large crowds. The debates reached a wide audience in their published form. Campbell's debate with Robert Owen (1771-1858), the Welsh skeptic and social reformer, made him a household name. In the debate, held in Cincinnati in 1829, Campbell's eloquent presentation of the traditional arguments for the existence of God established his reputation as the Protestant champion of the Christian faith, standing against the destructive force of European free thought.

His reputation as a Protestant leader increased with later debates. In 1837, also in Cincinnati, Campbell debated Bishop John B. Purcell of the Roman Catholic Church. The discussion mainly dealt with issues surrounding public education. Campbell defended the Protestant character of public schooling against Purcell's promotion of parochial schools. A good number of Protestant leaders took notice of his eloquence in defending their cause. But Campbell also

Campbell's debate with Robert Owen (1771-1858)

enjoyed debating fellow Protestants. In 1843, in Lexington, Kentucky, he engaged Presbyterian minister N. L. Rice. This debate, one that resulted in more published pages than any other, dealt with issues quite specific to the Disciples, like believer's immersion versus infant baptism and the weekly celebration of the Lord's Supper.

Of course, Alexander Campbell was not the only leader to have debates or publish papers and books. But these activities greatly increased his influence. Through his monthly periodicals, occasional pamphlets, a Bible translation, hymnbooks, published debates, and other books, he proclaimed the basic principles, set the boundaries, and dealt with specific issues for the early movement. Through these endeavors, he gave form and direction to a largely congregationally oriented church that had no central organization.

BECOMING ORGANIZED FOR MISSIONS

Most of the evangelistic activities of the early movement empha-sized "capsizing" Baptists and others, as Raccoon John Smith once put it, inviting them to become "Christians only." This approach naturally resulted from their early understanding that successful Christian unity rested on an ability to recover "that simple original form of Christianity." Disciples called other Christians to join them in this task.

It took some time for Disciples to organize what might be described as world mission. For nearly two decades following their union in 1832, the Christians (Stone's churches) and the Reformers or Disciples (Campbell's churches) had their hands full trying to organize an emerging unified movement. Their congregational organization further created difficulty for the development of inter-national mission work, since few single congregations could sup-port a missionary. In the early days of the *Christian Baptist*, Alexander Campbell had written against missionary societies, claiming the early church worked only through its local capacity.

By the 1840s, Campbell had changed his mind. He now led a movement gaining influence in the larger culture. Campbell felt Disciples would not reach their full potential for service without a cooperative organization among the congregations. From 1842-1848, he penned a series of articles in the *Millennial Harbinger* on church cooperation, eventually calling for a church-wide organiza-tion to promote missions.

As early as 1829, church leaders in local areas had met to share information and encouragement. By 1844, regular statewide meet-ings had occurred in Kentucky, Ohio, Indiana, and Tennessee. The first organizations formed in response to the call for church-wide support among the Disciples were the American Christian Bible Society, begun in 1845, and the Sunday School and Tract Society, begun in 1846. David S. Burnet (1808-1867), twenty years younger than Campbell, led both organizations and also took the initiative in beginning a new missionary society.

Campbell had called for a general convention of the Disciples in Cincinnati in November 1849. Leaders hoped each congregation would send delegates to the convention, but many congregations did not participate and individuals simply came on their own. The convention ended up being a mass meeting of 156 members from about one hundred churches and eleven states rather than a truly representative body. Out of this meeting came the American Christian Missionary Society (ACMS), with Alexander Campbell chosen as its first president (although Campbell himself was not present due to illness).

The right of the ACMS to exist eventually became a divisive issue among Disciples, contributing to the split between Disciples of Christ and Churches of Christ. But, from its beginning, the society played an important role in sending the first Disciple missionaries from the United States to other countries.

Since Peter first preached the gospel in Jerusalem according to Acts, Disciples wanted to send their first foreign missionary to that city. Disciples generally shared the Protestant millennial belief of the time that the Jews needed to be converted before Christ could return to end history. They chose James T. Barclay (1807-1874), a well-educated physician, and his wife Julia, for the task. The Barclays had two tours of duty in Jerusalem, 1850-1854 and 1858-1861. They were not, however, very suitably prepared. They knew nothing of the languages spoken there and understood very little of the culture. While their work led to a few Christian converts, it left no lasting church.

The Barclays received criticism from many in the society because they participated in the practice of slavery. Shortly after they left for Jerusalem, a congregation in Hopkinsville, Kentucky, bought the freedom of Alexander Cross, a black preacher. The ACMS sent him as a missionary to newly freed blacks who had been sent to Liberia. Cross left for Liberia in 1854, but died of fever two months after his arrival. The only early mission that had even modest success was that of the third society missionary, J. O. Beardslee (1814-1879), who worked in Jamaica from 1858-1866.

Since these were the only missionaries sent by the ACMS before the Civil War, one is tempted to call its efforts a failure. Yet, what may be most significant about the ACMS is not what it accomplished in missions but what it said about the developing identity of the Disciples. From two small fellowships in 1832, the church had grown through evangelism, education, and publications to be a formidable religious body, capable of organizing even for international action.

The Movement Takes Root in Canada

The first indications of what became the Canadian Stone-Campbell Movement were evident in the Maritime Provinces (New Brunswick, Nova Scotia, and Prince Edward Island) by 1810. Most of the early leaders there (John R. Stewart, Alexander Crawford, James Murray, and John Stevenson) had some connection to Scotland, either to the Scotch Baptists or to the Haldanes. Their early congregations emphasized restoring the early church, immersion of believers, and a weekly offering of the Lord's Supper. Not

75

yet connected formally to Disciples, they sounded common themes that enabled later connections with the movement. By the 1820s, an American named William W. Ashley married a Canadian and carried Campbell's writings to Halifax, Nova Scotia. In the 1830s, as disagreements arose among Baptists in the Maritimes, some of the Scotch Baptist congregations established connections with the Stone-Campbell oriented congregation in Halifax. By the 1850s, a formal association of Christian churches emerged in the Maritimes.

Scotch Baptists, most of whom were associated with the Haldanes in Scotland, also immigrated to southwestern Ontario between 1818 and 1820. In addition, several congregations associated with the Christian Connection (see Chapter Two) developed during the 1820s on the northern side of Lake Ontario. When these congregations refused to unify with the Disciples in the United States in 1834, one of the ministers present, Joseph Ash, decided to establish the first Disciples congregation in Ontario at Cobourg in 1836. By 1843, some twenty-four congregations associated with Disciples existed in Ontario. A few of the developing leaders, including David Oliphant Jr. and Edmund Sheppard, made their way to Bethany to study with Campbell. Oliphant helped to spread Disciples views through his work as an editor of the *Witness of Truth*. In 1855, Alexander Campbell visited Ontario, traveling from Niagara Falls in the east to London in the west. He met with leaders, preached in a variety of churches, including both Methodist and Baptist churches, and helped to cement relations with the growing number of Disciples in Canada. Disciples developments in the Prairies, further west in Canada, took place in later decades.

THE ROLE OF WOMEN IN THE EARLY STONE-CAMPBELL MOVEMENT

The culture of the United States in the first half of the nineteenth century did not encourage leadership roles for women. The ethos of most Protestant groups not only mirrored this cultural reality, but also largely contributed to its strength. However, educational opportunities for women were improving as the century wore on and, increasingly, women were finding their voice in demanding a larger role in both society and church. In some respects, the congregational organization and authority that characterized Disciples life helped to increase opportunities for women compared to the hierarchical church machinery that operated in many of the more established Christian denominations. The nature of popular religion, so fully embraced by Disciples as they grew, also helped facilitate a more important role for women. Further, an understanding of ministry that emphasized God's call and a recognition of personal gifts for ministry also helped women gain a more distinctive place among Disciples congregations.

Like most of the leaders of the Protestant churches of his day, Alexander Campbell went on record fairly early, speaking against women taking a leading role in congregations and in ministry. But in spite of Campbell's negative statements, a few women were involved in preaching, the organization of churches, and performing baptisms for new Christians.

Some of these early women leaders had been connected to either James O'Kelly's movement, to the Christian Connection, or to Baptist or Quaker roots. Joseph Thomas, an early minister associated with the Stone Christians, noted in his autobiography (1812) the powerful preaching of a Kentucky woman, who was most likely Nancy Mulkey, the daughter of John Mulkey, another preacher associated with Stone churches. Three women, loosely associated with the Baptists of the Redstone Association, Mary T. Graft, Mary Morrison, and Mary Ogle, began evangelizing house to house, eventually creating a church in Somerset, Pennsylvania. They affiliated with the Campbells after a visit from Thomas Campbell around 1828. The church grew to more than five hundred members. Another prominent woman leader, Mary Stogdill, originally baptized in Greenville, New York, emerged as a leader early in the Canadian movement's history. She preached, baptized, recruited ministers and helped to form the Christian Conference in Ontario in 1821. The role of women among Disciples, as we shall see, became much more prominent following the Civil War.

For Further Reading

Butchart, Reuben. *The Disciples of Christ in Canada since 1830.* Toronto: Canadian Headquarters' Publications, Churches of Christ (Disciples), 1949.

Cummins, D. Duane. *The Disciples: A Struggle for Reformation.* St. Louis: Chalice Press, 2009. See pages 80-97.

Garrett, Leroy. *The Stone-Campbell Movement.* Joplin, Mo.: College Press, 1994. See pages 143-172.

Hull, Debra Beery. *Christian Church Women: Shapers of a Movement.* St. Louis: Chalice Press, 1994.

Toulouse, Mark G., ed. *Walter Scott: A Nineteenth Century Evangelical.* St. Louis: Chalice Press, 1999.

Webb, Henry E. *In Search of Christian Unity.* 1990; new edition, Abilene: Abilene Christian University Press, 2003.

Questions for Discussion

1. What was Walter Scott's greatest contribution to the Disciples?

2. What were the six points Scott used to summarize the gospel? Compare Scott's presentation of the gospel with that of contemporary Disciple theologian Clark Williamson in the Introduction. How would you define the gospel?

3. List some of the early colleges founded by members of the Stone-Campbell Movement. How did these colleges serve the early Disciples churches?

4. List some of the religious papers in the early movement. How did these serve the early congregations?

5. How did the Disciples start the work in Canada?

6. Who were the first three international missionaries of the movement? Where were they sent? How were they supported? What does this say about the movement in the late 1800s?

DEVELOPING A THEOLOGY

"Theology" was a bad word among the early Disciples. Barton Stone, Alexander Campbell, and all the other early Restoration leaders largely avoided the term. To them "theology" seemed more like divisive speculation. Theology, particularly as expressed in the detailed creeds of their day, divided Christians. They wanted Christ to unite them, and efforts to espouse human theology tended to divide.

Today's Disciples define theology as "reflection about God and our relation to God" and to assert that all Christians have a theology. Campbell and others were right to point out that faith in God, not in theology, is the mark of the Christian. These early leaders, however, did express a thoughtful faith. They had a particular approach to Christianity, shaped by their time and experience. So do we. So do all Christians. We all have a theology. The question is, will it be a well-thought-out theology, or will we thoughtlessly accept what others tell us about the faith? Actually, the early Restoration leaders actively opposed just this kind of mindless acceptance of traditionalism.

In a brief space, this chapter cannot fully discuss the complete theology of early Disciples. Instead, we will focus on three aspects of the thought of Alexander Campbell that, in some measure, still influence the theological expressions of contemporary Disciples: his view of the early church and unity, his approach to understanding the Bible, and his view of baptism and what it means to be a Christian.

UNITY AND THE EARLY CHURCH

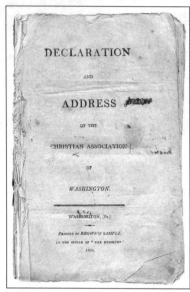

DECLARATION

AND

ADDRESS

OF THE

CHRISTIAN ASSOCIATION

OF

WASHINGTON.

WASHINGTON, (Pa.)

PRINTED BY BROWN & SAMPLE,
AT THE OFFICE OF "THE REPORTER"
1809.

Declaration and Address

At the heart of early Disciples theology is the desire to restore to the church important elements it had lost through the ages, especially its unity. As we saw in Chapter Four, when Thomas Campbell penned the *Declaration and Address* in 1809, his primary theme was the unity of the church: "Prop. 1. That the Church of Christ upon earth is essentially, intentionally, and constitutionally one." Thomas Campbell believed the church could enjoy that unity if it would leave behind the doctrines that divided Christians in order to practice those teachings "expressly exhibited" in the New Testament. That phrase and others such as "plain," "clear," "manifest," "simple," and "original pattern" occur more than sixty times in the *Declaration and Address*. To Thomas Campbell the essentials of the faith and the shape of the church should be plain to all. Of course, all of history indicates that the essentials are murkier than leaders in the nineteenth century supposed. The clarity of essentials often depends on factors that influence one's reading of the Bible.

While Thomas Campbell never spelled out exactly what the express shape of the church should be, his son, Alexander Campbell, was not so reticent. In a series of thirty articles on "A Restoration of the Ancient Order of Things," published in the *Christian Baptist* between 1825 and 1829, Alexander attempted to lay out the original pattern of the church.

The content of most of Campbell's articles is not surprising. Five of the articles deal with general principles of restoration. Two list the dangers of creeds. Nine of the thirty articles are on worship, with four arguing for weekly communion. Five articles are on church offices: bishop, deacon, and others.

What might surprise some who unfairly characterize Campbell as an unfeeling rationalist are the two articles on the "Spirit and Temper of Mind of the Ancient Order," and "Devotion to God's Will" where Campbell recounts his own religious experience. Perhaps surprising to contemporary church members are his seven articles on "Church Discipline." Campbell believed the church had a role in disciplining errant members who failed to represent Christian principles fully in their own lives. The purpose of restoring the ancient order was not to be legalistically correct, but to make the church a school of discipleship and devotion to Christ. For Campbell, the concept of restoration also meant to recognize that the church belongs to God, not to us. Therefore, its members should seek to keep the church free from either human self-interest or the tendency toward self-righteousness. The church must seek its direction from God. The model of the early church in the pages of the Bible provided some help in that regard.

Why did the Campbells speak so much about the church to the neglect of other doctrines? Did they think doctrines about God, Christ, the Holy Spirit, salvation, and last things were less important than the church? No. Both Campbells had a broad theological and classical education and could place the doctrine of the church in a broader theological context. And they always did. However, they sought to understand the nature of the church and God's mission for it in the world, because the church seemed to be terribly divided in their time.

Both Thomas and Alexander Campbell believed that most Protestant bodies in their day understood foundational Christian doctrines appropriately. But the life of the church seemed to be in trouble, threatened by division largely resulting from human additions and requirements. The Campbells wanted to remove unwanted additions to the church and restore to it aspects that had been lost through the years. They sought "to bring the Christianity and the church of the present up to the New Testament standard." They judged much of the Christianity of their day to be sound and original. They generally agreed with Protestants about their views of God and Christ. Yet they understood as deficient much of the Protestant expression of the church. The church needed restoring in order to recover its original unity. And above all things, early

Disciples emphasized that Christians should be able to live in unity with one another as the one church.

Alexander Campbell's treatment of the Apostles' Creed clearly reveals his approach. Although he consistently opposed creeds as tests of fellowship, he nevertheless says, "We never objected to a creed properly so called. We have a creed—an apostolic creed." He then quotes the Apostles' Creed and adds to it baptism for remission of sins, weekly communion, and other "facts or articles of belief." Campbell did not emphasize the basic articles of the Apostles' Creed, even though he thought them central in importance, because the churches of his day already believed them. Instead, he focused on those areas the church still lacked. In restoring an old house, one can ignore the foundation if it is sound. That does not make it less important but less in need of urgent attention.

This explains why theology among Disciples is not so much thin as uneven and spotty. Historically, Disciples have overemphasized some doctrines at the expense of others that were as important, if not more important. The doctrine of the church is one area where Disciples theology has been strong, so strong in fact, that in the middle decades of the twentieth century it eclipsed all other doctrines among Disciples, resulting in a restructured church that did not always express well its own theological sense of the marks of Christian faith.

This early view of restoration has other implications. It implies that restoration is an ongoing process. The early Disciples viewed the work of restoring the church as one not likely to stop before the end of time. The early idea of restoration was also not an end in itself. Restoration was for the purpose of unity, and seeking unity served the purpose of restoration. Later some Disciples felt that one must choose between restoration and unity. Our early leaders felt they should always go together—that unity would bring restoration, and restoration would bring unity.

Today's Disciples are not quite so quick to affirm two of the presuppositions the founders had with regard to the early church and its unity. First, contemporary Disciples are more likely to recognize that the earliest congregations were themselves diverse. Nineteenth-century Disciples were confident that local gatherings of the faithful were united in essential matters of "doctrine, worship, discipline, and government," as Thomas Campbell expressed it. And that all these things were perfectly expressed in those early communities. Today, Disciples are more inclined to recognize that the church is always historically situated—that there has never been a golden age for the church. A theological understanding for today's Disciples generally includes the belief that the church is always affected by human sin. The church works to express perfectly the will of God in history, but always falls short of actually getting there. Historically, the early church developed in its self-understanding. It inherited characteristics from its surroundings, from Jewish, Greek, and Roman ideas. As Acts clearly indicates, the congregation in Antioch held to different views and practices than the church in Jerusalem.

Second, Disciples now understand the church to be a living, breathing institution that, by virtue of its very existence, must interact with history itself. The church adapts and changes and is necessarily found in a variety of expressions across the globe. Rather than an unchanging institution that is always and everywhere the same, across all time, the church represents the kind of vitality that is theologically associated with the Spirit of God. There is no singular mold or model for the church that can be restored. Therefore, unity is not to be accomplished around a static notion of the church, but rather in the midst of a dynamic, ever-changing church. Unity cannot succeed without the awareness that it should (and must) exist among very different manifestations of church found in vastly differing Christian communities across the world. Disciples today stress the importance of affirming unity with others while standing in the midst of radical diversity.

When the church does connect meaningfully with the purposes of God in human history, it does so in necessarily human and impermanent ways. Recognizing this truth does not mean the church does not do significant work, but rather helps to keep the church from becoming self-righteous and self-interested so that it can perform meaningful ministry within the world.

INTERPRETING THE BIBLE

Alexander Campbell offers his method of biblical interpretation in his book, *The Christian System*. His rules reflect common sense and the biblical scholarship of his time. His approach had its roots in the Enlightenment enterprise that sought to free the Bible from sectarian strife by reading it scientifically, that is, grammatically and historically, as one would read any other book. He thus bequeathed to his followers a strong historical approach to scripture. But he is not a thoroughgoing Enlightenment rationalist. Indeed, his most important, "indispensable" rule is: "We must come within the understanding distance." One may follow all the rules of reason and still not hear God in scripture. To understand truly, one must be "ravished with the moral scenes that the Bible unfolds." One must have "one ardent desire—intent only to know the will of God."

Campbell regarded the heart as the seat of our deepest moral intentions, giving it preeminence over reason. Christians must read the Bible with more than the mind. True, Campbell sometimes spoke as if he equated heart with mind, but a close reading of his work shows he transcended the strict rationalism of his day by giving precedence to obedience from the heart over understanding with the mind. He called for pious scholars who put the word into practice.

Campbell's hermeneutic (his method of biblical interpretation) was also Christocentric. He taught that one should use the best contemporary methods of Bible interpretation, but must always keep the focus on relationship to Christ. This prevents his hermeneutic from becoming fixed and legalistic. Later, some Disciples developed a more narrow hermeneutic focusing on what practices the Bible authorizes. While the early restoration leaders certainly felt that rightly handling the scriptures and arriving at correct teaching was important, they all stressed the Bible's portrait of Christ as word of God more than any specific strategy of interpretation.

Yet, their tendency to view the Bible as "constitution" did encourage early Disciples to understand the practices of the church they uncovered in it as a blueprint for their time. Later in the nineteenth century, new developments in biblical interpretation led many Disciples to take a different view of biblical authority. While affirming their dependence on the Bible for understanding God and the work of Christ, later Disciples recognized they could not read the Bible literally. The revelation of God always travels through human sources and is, to some degree, entangled in both history and the cultural views of its authors. Scriptural views of women or slavery, for example, are more representative of the second century than they are any kind of biblical mandate applicable in the twenty-first century.

Disciples in the generations following Campbell remained a people of the book. Like Campbell, the biblical critics late in the century believed in applying the best available methods of biblical interpretation to its pages. For these Disciples, the Bible, in their developing view, led them to an experience of the revelation of God, but is not, in itself, the revelation of God. The narratives found in its pages direct readers to an awareness of God and an experience of Christ. But for these later Disciples, the authority of the Bible rests more in the spirit of its message than in a literal application of its words.

BAPTISM AND SECTARIANISM

More than any other teaching, the early leader's insistence on believer's immersion for forgiveness of sins set them apart from other Christian groups. Even Baptists, who practiced believer's immersion, did not emphasize baptism's connection to the formal remission of sins.

Early in the history of the Disciples, some wondered if this emphasis on baptism would become divisive and sectarian. In 1830 Barton Stone worried that insisting on immersion could become a one-item sectarian creed that would exclude more Christians from union than any creed in existence. With some in the movement, this fear would become a reality. They would exclude all the unimmersed from the very name "Christian."

In 1837, an unnamed woman from Lunenburg, Virginia, wrote Alexander Campbell expressing her surprise at his statement that he found Christians in all the Protestant groups. Campbell printed the letter in the *Millennial Harbinger* because it allowed him to answer several questions: Are only immersed believers entitled to the name Christian? Are all the Christians in the world in Campbell's Movement? Can we call the unimmersed "Christians" and still insist they be immersed?

In his reply, Campbell spoke clearly: there must be Christians among the Protestant sects. Otherwise, he argued, there would have been no Christians in the world for centuries and Jesus' promise that

85

THE

MILLENNIAL HARBINGER.

EDITED BY

ALEXANDER CAMPBELL.

I saw another messenger flying through the midst of heaven, having everlasting good news to proclaim to the inhabitants of the earth, even to every nation and tribe, and tongue, and people—saying with a loud voice, Fear God and give glory to him, for the hour of his judgments is come: and worship him who made heaven, and earth, and sea, and the fountains of water.—JOHN. Great is the truth and mighty above all things, and will prevail.

VOL. I.

BETHANY, VA.
PRINTED AND PUBLISHED BY THE EDITOR
1830.

Millennial Harbinger

the gates of hell would not prevail against the church (Matthew 16:18) would have proved false. Campbell said, "This cannot be; and therefore there are Christians among the sects."

The plea for unity, to "come out" of sectarianism, itself implies that there are Christians in the denominations. If all the Christians in the world were already united in the Stone-Campbell churches, then why would Campbell and others call Christians to come out of their sectarianism? In other words, to plead for unity necessarily means there are Christians to unify. Unfortunately, there were some even in Campbell's day who thought he wished to "make and lead a large exclusivist party" who claimed to be the only Christians. He vehemently denied this, saying, "I think there are many, in most Protestant parties, whose errors and mistakes I hope the Lord will forgive."

Some have tried to paint Alexander Campbell as inconsistent on this issue, claiming the "early Campbell" was a strict restorationist who saw his followers (or perhaps all the immersed) as the only Christians, while the "later Campbell" abandoned that position and became more ecumenical. Campbell himself refutes this charge by quoting his writings from the early years to show that he had always believed there are Christians among the other denominations.

The belief that there are Christians among the other churches raises the question of baptism. As the Lunenburg letter asks, "What act of yours gave you the name of Christian?" In his preaching, his writing, and his debates, Campbell had strongly defended believers' immersion as the biblical form of baptism and had called on those baptized as infants to be immersed as adults. This emphasis led some of his followers to assume that only the immersed were Christians. They were shocked to find Campbell calling at least some of the unimmersed "Christians," and they accused him of abandoning his position on the importance of biblical baptism.

86

He replied by accusing some of his correspondents of being "ultraists," that is, legalists, on the subject of baptism. They had made baptism itself a savior, claiming it was the single standard by which one is judged to be a Christian. Campbell never taught such "water salvation." He refused to make even immersion the single standard of Christian faith and character. If forced to choose between one baptized as an infant and one immersed as a believer, he preferred the one who loved Christ most, saying, "Did I act otherwise, I would be a pure sectarian, a Pharisee among Christians."

Although baptism is important, Campbell wrote, it is not more important than Christian character. To deny the name Christian to those who display the character of Christ is to be the worst kind of sectarian. It is to promote the legalistic, exclusivist barriers that Campbell worked all his life to tear down.

So, if the unimmersed are Christians, does that mean immersion is not essential for salvation and is relatively unimportant? No, Campbell says, baptism is still "unto salvation." How then can the unimmersed be Christians? Campbell's answer is that some of the unimmersed who were baptized as infants have never thought to inquire whether their baptism was scriptural, but took it for granted. Paul talks of one who does not have outward circumcision, but has inward circumcision. In the same way, Campbell asks, "Can a person who simply, not perversely, mistakes the outer baptism, have the inward?"

Campbell strongly denied that admitting there may be Christians among the sects detracts from the importance of baptism. He saw himself steering a middle course between essentialists and non-essentialists on baptism. He claimed he did not detract from the authority of baptism simply by admitting the possibility of one being Christian without it.

So, if Campbell believed one could be Christian without immersion, did he advocate open membership in the church and an easy-going ecumenism? No. Obedience to Christ and his ordinances (including baptism) were under usual conditions connected to Christian identity. In this, Campbell claims to agree with all Christians, Catholic and Protestant, who believe one who willfully disdains or neglects baptism is not Christian.

But one can act faithfully only to the extent of his or her knowledge. For Campbell, if one did not know baptism is believer's immersion, then one could not act faithfully. However, one who knew and rejected the ordinance was without excuse. Campbell told all who would listen to him that immersion for the forgiveness of sins constituted scriptural baptism. He required it for anyone who wished to be recognized as a member of a Disciples congregation. He did not downplay baptism to increase numbers. Neither did he judge the unimmersed to be outside the Christian fold.

Contemporary Disciples have emphasized that Campbell approached baptism from a careful reading of the New Testament and from within a Reformed theological perspective. For him, God's grace in salvation stood paramount. In response to God's grace, Campbell believed, Christians should respond faithfully in baptism. In this respect, contemporary Disciples baptismal understanding is a return to Campbell's emphasis on grace. In recent decades, Disciples have also recognized that the New Testament witness is a bit more complex than a believer's immersion only approach might readily recognize (i.e., 1 Cor. 1:10-17). Occasionally, entire "households" were baptized. The discovery of the early second-century document, the *Didache*, just seven years after Campbell's death, also revealed that the church practiced varying forms of baptism in its earliest history.

Responding to a developing ecumenical consensus on baptism, Disciples moved to recognize both infant baptism and believers' baptism as legitimate Christian practices. While one emphasizes God's grace and the other emphasizes human response, both together provide a witness to the fullness of meaning associated with baptism. Therefore, most Disciples congregations continue to practice believers' baptism as their standard form of baptism, but they usually accept Christians into full membership who have been baptized as infants. Disciples, in documents affirmed by the General Assembly, have urged that congregations should never encourage or engage in the practice of rebaptism. Disciples affirm that baptism is a one-time event, whether received as an infant or later as one who expresses Christian faith and requests baptism. When Disciples congregations receive families with small children who have been baptized as infants, those congregations generally nurture the Christian development of those children to enable them, eventually, to express their personal commitment to Christian faith.

Theology Then and Now

In summary, Campbell's influence remains in all these areas. Disciples continue to believe in the importance of the apostolic witness of faith, and in seeking to find ways to express more sub-stantially the unity of all Christians. Disciples produce their fair share of biblical scholars, and their ministers seek to utilize the best of contemporary scholarship to understand scripture and to preach its message. Most also remain Christocentric. They understand the dynamic witness of Christ as the truly authoritative revelation in human history, and the Christian basis for experiencing a meaningful relationship with God. Disciples continue to baptize, primarily through believers' immersion, as an expression of faith, but recognize Christians, accepting them as full members in their own congregations, who have been baptized using other forms. In these and other areas, a twenty-first century church can still learn from the ideals of the nineteenth-century Disciples.

For Further Reading

For the text of Alexander Campbell's discussion of the Lunenburg Letter, see *The Millennial Harbinger* (1836), p. 132.

Boring, M. Eugene. *Disciples and the Bible: A History of Disciples Biblical Interpretation in North America*. St. Louis: Chalice Press, 1997.

Heltzel, Peter Goodwin. *Chalice Introduction to Disciples Theology*. St. Louis: Chalice Press, 2008.

Jones, Serene. *Feminist Theory and Christian Theology: Cartographies of Grace*. Minneapolis: Augsburg Fortress, 2000.

Lawrence, Kenneth, ed. *Classic Themes of Disciple Theology*. Fort Worth: Texas Christian University Press, 1986.

Richesin, L. Dale and Bouchard, Larry D., eds. *Interpreting Disciples: Practical Theology in the Disciples of Christ*. Fort Worth: Texas Christian University Press, 1987.

Sprinkle, Stephen V. *Disciples and Theology*. St. Louis: Chalice Press, 1999.

Toulouse, Mark G., *Joined in Discipleship: The Shaping of Contemporary Disciples Identity*. St. Louis: Chalice Press, 1997. See pages 37-54, 73-100, and 137-162.

QUESTIONS FOR DISCUSSION

1. Is "theology" a good word or a bad word to you? Does a contemporary Disciples understanding of the word bring greater clarity for your thinking about the meaning of theology?

2. Why did the Campbells teach so much on the church to the neglect of other doctrines? Should Disciples today have the same emphasis on the church or have times changed? What is the difference between how Disciples think about the church and how Campbell thought about it?

3. What was Alexander Campbell's approach to hermeneutics (understanding the Bible)? Does this approach work today? What are its strengths and weaknesses? How do Disciples approach the Bible today?

4. What did the early Stone-Campbell leaders mean when they said, "Christians only, not the only Christians?" Does accepting others as Christians mean Disciples should abandon their emphasis on believer's immersion?

5. Why do contemporary Disciples accept infant baptism as a legitimate Christian baptism?

CHAPTER 8

THE GREAT DIVIDE OF THE CIVIL WAR

Until the last forty years or so, almost every history of the Stone-Campbell Movement denied any division during the Civil War. Other bodies like the Methodists, Baptists, and Presbyterians suffered division into northern and southern groups, but not Disciples, or so the story went. Moses Lard (1818-1880), a prominent Missouri preacher and editor, had urged members of the churches to refuse to fight in the war. Christians should avoid entanglement in such divisive political matters. In 1866, Lard admitted in his quarterly journal that the war had "cooled many an ardent feeling and caused old friends to regard one another a little shyly." Yet in the end, he insisted, the war had caused no division in Disciples ranks.

Lard's remarks have more to do with his notions of unity and division among Christians than they do with the Civil War. Still, his declaration that we had not divided carried the day for generations. His statement deserves reexamination, however, because the sectional feelings burned into the American mind by the events surrounding that terrible war shaped Disciples as much as they did all other Americans.

Moses Lard

91

SLAVERY AND THE CHURCHES

In 1860, there were about 1200 congregations in the North and about 800 in the South. Many were in border states like Kentucky, Ohio, and Missouri where differences over the issues that led to war were especially strong. Though many difficult political and social issues fueled the conflict, slavery and race stood at its heart. Members of the churches of the Stone-Campbell Movement were just as much a part of the heated discussions as anyone. Their attitudes about blacks and slavery reflected the same spectrum as the rest of America.

Both Barton W. Stone and Alexander Campbell opposed slavery, but Campbell also opposed abolitionism—the immediate freeing of all slaves by law—while Stone offered some support as early as the 1830s. Both men owned slaves at different times in their lives. Stone freed all his slaves by 1804, but later the law prevented him from emancipating several others he inherited from his wife's mother. He was a supporter of the American Colonization Society for several years. This group planned to end slavery over time by buying those enslaved from masters and sending them "back" to the West African nation of Liberia, purchased and established by the society for that purpose.

Campbell detailed his position on slavery in 1845 in a series of eight articles published in the *Millennial Harbinger* entitled "Our Position to American Slavery." The Methodist and Baptist Churches had just divided over slavery, and the debate over the annexation of Texas to the Union as a slave state threatened a major crisis in the nation and among Disciples.

Campbell spent considerable time explaining why the issue of slavery must not divide the churches. Though opposed to the institution, he appeared to be defending its existence in most of the articles. Nowhere in the Bible, he claimed, is the relation of master to slave sinful and immoral in itself. On the contrary, scripture seeks to regulate the relationship, not abolish it. When he finally began to explain why he opposed the practice, he attributed his opposition to, in his words, a matter of expediency. Sounding much like his fellow Virginian Thomas Jefferson, Campbell insisted that in the civilized world slavery was simply not in harmony with the spirit of the age or the advancement of society. A hindrance to personal and national prosperity, slavery imposed so many burdens on Christian owners that it worked against the kind of domestic happiness everyone really wanted. He described a gradual approach as the best way to end slavery without causing disruption to the nation and its institutions.

Not primarily interested in the welfare of those enslaved, Campbell expressed more interest in the unity of his reform movement. He regarded the conflict over slavery as a potential threat. His series of articles concluded with the assertion that "no Christian community, governed by the Bible, can constitutionally and rightfully make the simple relation of master and slave a term of Christian fellowship or a subject of discipline."

Campbell's attempt to state a "moderate" position that would de-fuse tension over the issue only seemed to anger people on both sides. John Kirk, a church leader in Ohio, wrote Campbell in 1851 that Disciples who enslaved others, after being admonished to free them, if they refused, "should be dealt with as we would with a horse thief or any other notorious villain." Kirk said that most of the members of the churches in his part of Ohio disagreed with Campbell on the subject of slavery. He ended his subscription to the *Millennial Harbinger* and stated he would not patronize any paper whose editor would not denounce the Fugitive Slave law and the government that passed it.

Pardee Butler (1816-1888) became, perhaps, the most outspoken abolitionist in the Stone-Campbell Movement. When he moved to Kansas in 1855 to work as an evangelist, his message was as much abolitionism as gospel. When the American Christian Missionary Society insisted that Butler stop preaching his anti-slavery views, a group of abolitionist church members from Ohio and Indiana formed a rival missionary society in 1859 that supported Butler until 1863.

Without question, the strongest pro-slavery voice in the Stone-Campbell Movement belonged to James Shannon (1799-1859). He asserted what many Disciples mistakenly took

Pardee Butler

93

for granted, that blacks were inferior and not capable of living responsibly as free people. Nature, the United States Constitution, and the Bible all clearly approved slavery, he said, and any attempt to violate the rights of masters to enslave others as legal property should be resisted even to the point of war.

Butler and Shannon represented the opposite ends of the spectrum on the issue. Many church members were content to take Campbell's position and stay out of the fights. However, that became almost impossible with the outbreak of the war in 1861. Opinions were most diverse and tensions greatest in the "border" states like Kentucky and Missouri. Just as with later divisive issues like instrumental music and missionary societies, the question of slavery became a matter each congregation had to work out for itself. Disciples did not have a national organization to facilitate the kind of division seen among the Baptists, Methodists, and Presbyterians. Or, on second thought, maybe they did.

THE CHURCHES IN THE CIVIL WAR

Though by no means working like a Presbyterian General Assembly or Methodist Conference, the Stone-Campbell Movement did have a national organization—the American Christian Missionary Society. Headquartered in the north, in Cincinnati, Ohio, the annual meetings had always enjoyed attendance from across the country. When the war began, southerners could no longer attend the meetings.

Just as many Disciples leaders had been "moderates" on the issue of slavery, many (led again by Campbell himself) refused to endorse either side in the war. It is not surprising, then, that outsiders began to question the loyalty to the Union of the missionary society and the churches it represented. At the October 1861 meeting, some members introduced a resolution calling on Disciples churches to do everything in their power to support the Union. The society itself did not adopt this resolution, since some insisted that political resolutions like this one were outside the legitimate business of the missionary society. So they called a ten-minute recess, voted on it as a mass meeting rather than as the society, and approved the resolution.

Technically, the American Christian Missionary Society did not pass the resolution. No matter. When word got back to southern church leaders what had happened, they reacted quickly. Tolbert Fanning in Nashville, Tennessee, had been urging southern Christians to stay out of the conflict. When he heard about the resolution, he took it to mean that the ACMS had begun encouraging supporters to join the Union armies and participate in the murder of people in the South. Unless those who had passed this resolution repented of what they had done, Fanning said he could no longer regard them as brothers.

David Lipscomb

But the worst had not yet come. The rumors about the society's early hesitancy to support the Union had not been squelched by the resolution. The abolitionists who had organized the rival missionary society continued their harsh criticism of the ACMS. In 1863, the society decided that it would put an end to these accusations once and for all. This time the society itself in session—no recess, no unofficial mass meeting—passed a much stronger resolution.

> Resolved, that we unqualifiedly declare our allegiance to [the United States] government, and repudiate as false and slanderous any statements to the contrary. That we tender our sympathies to our brave and noble soldiers in the field who are defending us from the attempts of armed traitors to overthrow our government . . . .

With these acts in 1861 and 1863, the American Christian Missionary Society aligned itself politically with the North. Though many church leaders in the North like Benjamin Franklin (1812-1878) had remained neutral throughout the war, the society had chosen sides in a political and military conflict. The man who would become the foremost church leader in the South after the Civil War, David Lipscomb (1831-1917), wrote in 1866 that the society had committed a great wrong against the church and the cause of God. Unless there is repentance of the wrong, he

95

asserted, "it should not receive the confidence of the Christian brotherhood."

This sectional division gave impetus to the revival of an old journal and the creation of a new one after the war. In 1866, the *Gospel Advocate*, published in Nashville, Tennessee, and edited by Tolbert Fanning and David Lipscomb, resumed publication. The war had forced it to shut down in 1861. Lipscomb revived it because southerners could read no other Disciples paper without being offended by "political insinuations and slurs." Though the editors denied they intended the *Advocate* to be a sectional paper, it clearly became a Southern journal—written by Southern leaders for Southern members.

After the war, a new paper also began publication in the North. A group of church and business leaders formed a publishing company to create the *Christian Standard*, a paper they believed would be more in keeping with the times. Previously, the *American Christian Review*, edited by Benjamin Franklin, had the most influence in the North. Unlike the leaders who formed the new company, Franklin had been neutral during the Civil War. Many Disciples considered him too narrow and legalistic, in other words, an "old fogy."

Like the *Gospel Advocate*, the sectional political feelings behind the *Christian Standard* were never part of the public explanation for starting the paper. But its sectional character remained clearly on display. In 1867, David Lipscomb met Isaac Errett, the first editor of the new paper. Years later, Lipscomb reported that Errett had admitted the *Standard* began because Franklin would not let the pro-union people publish their beliefs that Christians should support the government in time of war.

Were Disciples Divided by the Civil War?

The notion that anyone in America before, during, and after the Civil War could have remained unaffected by such a momentous event is remarkably naive. The war created two very different moods in the country—one in the North and one in the South—that no one could escape. Northerners had won the war. There was a general sense of victory, progress, and prosperity, mixed with a desire to punish or rehabilitate the South. Southerners had been defeated. To survive, they interpreted their defeat as discipline from

God to keep them from becoming like the materialistic North and to preserve their virtues as an example of God's ideal culture.

Thus, not just the war but also its aftermath, particularly Reconstruction in the South, broke Christian fellowship. After the war, many churches in the prosperous northern cities became successful in society. They built large buildings with expensive stained glass. They preferred educated ministers. They could even afford expensive organs for their new buildings. Indeed, as we shall see, some opposed instrumental music in worship more for its "worldliness" than because they thought it "unscriptural." The Disciples in the North actually became connected enough to the mainline aspects of culture that an itinerant preacher in their midst, James A. Garfield (1831-1881), became President of the United States.

By contrast, many Disciples in the South faced starvation, disease, and economic ruin. Although some Northern church leaders made the effort to raise humanitarian support for the South, little aid actually arrived. Southerners could not understand how their fellow Disciples in the North could spend money on buildings and organs while Disciples in the South were struggling just to stay alive.

Did the Civil War divide Disciples? Certainly not in the same way it divided the Baptists, Methodists, and Presbyterians. Disciples did not have the same kind of central organization that represented and acted for the churches as a whole. Nevertheless, Disciples did have structures, like the American Christian Missionary Society, and Disciples also had newspapers. Though less formal than official assemblies and conferences, these organizations embodied the division that had taken place in the minds and hearts of Christians in the North and in the South.

The Civil War divided Disciples in another way as well. Black Disciples, in order to exercise their gifts as leaders in the church, began to form separate congregations. In some locations, white Disciples helped black Disciples form their own congregations because a separate church life made sense to them at the time. During this period, black Disciples acted to fulfill their God-given gifts in any way they could. Some of these separate congregations remained connected to the main body of Disciples. Others did not. Thus, white Disciples found themselves divided in congregations largely along ethnic lines. But they also had provided the impetus for a more complete rupture in their church life.

A separate movement of black Disciples emerged along the eastern seaboard of the country, originating in the eastern region of North Carolina. Known as the Black Disciple Assemblies, these congregations adopted some of the characteristics associated with the Free Will Baptists. A good many of the white congregations in this region that had affiliated with Disciples had originally been Free Will Baptist congregations that had practiced foot-washing as an ordinance. In the period before the Civil War, these congregations had included black members as well. As the black congregations formed, many of them carried the practice of foot-washing forward into the next century as a sacrament. The earliest of these congregations was the Free Union church of Christ at Uniontown, formed in 1854 out of a previously racially mixed Disciples congregation known as Welche's Creek Church. This congregation, located in North Carolina, became known as the "mother church" of the Black Disciple Assemblies congregations. As new congregations were formed, they connected in an association of their own, having little reason to connect with white church structures. The Black Disciples Assemblies, formed from these developments, remains an active church body today, related significantly to Disciples history, but separated from the main body of Disciples of Christ.

The North-South division among Disciples remained real and substantial. The 1906 U.S. Census of Religious Bodies, published in 1909, formally recognized the division between two forms of the Stone-Campbell Movement. When the dust settled, about eighty-three percent of the Disciples of Christ lived in the North and two-thirds of the Churches of Christ lived in the South. The war definitely divided Disciples. But other factors also divided them.

For Further Reading

Cummins, D. Duane. *The Disciples: A Struggle for Reformation*. St. Louis: Chalice Press, 2009. See pages 112-123.

Garrett, Leroy. *The Stone-Campbell Movement*. Joplin, Mo.: College Press, 1994. See pages 333-355.

Gillams, Sheila Hope. "Principle and Practice: The Quandary of African American Restorationists in the History and Theology of the Church of Christ, Disciples of Christ, 1850-1950." Ph.D. diss., Union Theological Seminary, New York City, 2002.

Harrell, David Edwin, Jr. *Quest for a Christian America: The Disciples of Christ and American Society to 1866*. Nashville: Disciples of Christ Historical Society, 1966. See pages 91-138.

North, James B. *Union in Truth: An Interpretive History of the Restoration Movement*. Cincinnati: Standard Publishing, 1994. See pages 227-252.

Poyner, Barry C. *Bound to Slavery: James Shannon and the Restoration Movement*. Ft. Worth: Star Bible Publications, 1999.

Toulouse, Mark G. *God in Public: Four Ways American Christianity and Public Life Relate*. Louisville: Westminister John Knox Press, 2006.

Questions for Discussion

1. Though Disciples, in some ways, divided over slavery, their struggles to deal with the issue eventually led them to affirm the importance of the equality of all races. In your view, is it important for Disciples to make connections between Christian faith and important contemporary public issues? Why or why not?

2. In what sense did the Stone-Campbell Movement avoid division during the Civil War era?

4. In what sense did the Stone-Campbell Movement divide during the Civil War era?

5. In what ways did the Civil War era lay the foundation for other divisions that would come later?

ISSUES AND EDITORS

How does one unite groups that possess very little organization beyond the congregations? That was the question in 1832 when the Stone and Campbell churches united. The answer then was two-fold: congregation by congregation through the work of travelling preachers and through the influence of religious papers. How does a congregational movement divide? Moses Lard and others believed the Disciples could not divide because they did not have the denominational structure to formalize a division. To some degree, the Missionary Society fulfilled this role as churches either supported or opposed it. But fundamentally Disciples divided as they united, congregation by congregation, through the influence of religious editors and powerful preachers.

What issues divided Disciples? Again, slavery, the Civil War, and Reconstruction were among the causes of division. The war and its consequences shaped the discussion of most of the religious issues in the division—the Missionary Society and instrumental music—as well as the approaches to biblical interpretation that stood behind those religious issues.

ADDITIONAL CULTURAL FACTORS IN THE DIVISION

Though the division of Disciples into two groups only became clear with the publication of the 1906 religious census, the sources of division reached back well into the 1800s, as illustrated by regional differences in the Disciples approach to slavery. From the beginning, the movement contained unusual alliances and tensions.

Educated leaders and uneducated travelling ministers worked together for the common plea. And then there was the plea itself, bringing together a desire to restore ancient beliefs and practices with a commitment to the unity of the church. Some insisted on certain fundamental early commitments, while others urged tolerance for the sake of unity. As the movement grew and created cooperative organizations to further its mission, the stress between these differences began to emerge and broaden.

As David Edwin Harrell has documented well, all the divisions of American culture—"North and South, East and West, urban and rural, affluent and dispossessed"—marked and divided Disciples from one another. Much more than the arguments surrounding Christian beliefs or practices, these kind of cultural differences lay behind most of the arguments and, ultimately, the rupture between Disciples and Churches of Christ.

In the South, Christians tended to link a conservative faith to Southern values. In the North, Christians sought a more sophisticated, often urban expression of faith. Southern preachers condemned Northern progressive innovations, while preachers in the North complained of the backward and primitive church life found in the South. Again, as Harrell's work has demonstrated, the 1936 religious census revealed that fully 70% of Disciples lived in cities, while 56% of the members of the Churches of Christ were located in rural congregations. Even in the South, most of the Disciples were found in the cities. The census also showed that church buildings related to the Churches of Christ were valued at around $3,000 compared to $16,000 for the Disciples of Christ.

Very clearly, economic factors also played an important part in the split between these two heirs of the Stone-Campbell Movement. As is fairly evident in what follows, all the so-called "doctrinal" issues in the division are connected to economic and other cultural factors. Disciples were located primarily in the wealthier North, often leaders in business and industry, and usually lived in the cities. Those connected to the Churches of Christ were more often agrarian, either poor or at least of more modest means, and not at all interested in the extravagance often associated with urban churches. In Christian circles like these, missionary societies and organs in churches seemed excessive, even lavish, considering the poverty they experienced all around them.

Opposition to the Missionary Society

When the American Christian Missionary Society was formed in Cincinnati in 1849, it encountered little opposition from preachers and editors in the church. Two of those who were later most vehement in their opposition—Tolbert Fanning and Benjamin Franklin—had even once served as officers of the society.

Tolbert Fanning

Among the first to break with the society, Tolbert Fanning began the *Gospel Advocate* in 1855. By 1857, Fanning had concluded that the Bible did not authorize the founding of a missionary society. Yet he refused at this point to break fellowship with those who supported the society. He even addressed the society's annual meeting in 1859, rejoicing that the movement remained united. But after the society's pro-Union resolutions in 1861 and 1863, Fanning believed association with the society justified a break in fellowship.

The same pattern holds with Benjamin Franklin, who edited the popular *American Christian Review* published in Cincinnati, the headquarters of the society. Franklin served as a secretary for the society for thirteen years, but in 1866 turned completely against it. Although from the North, he felt scandalized by the society's abandonment of neutrality and pacifism during the war.

The arguments against the society were generally consistent among those who opposed it. It had become involved in sectional politics. It represented an inefficient way to do mission work. The society created financial expenses and its meetings meant traveling and restaurants and hotels. Who had the money for such things? The leadership of the society tended to dictate to the churches. Why did they assume to know what was best for congregations they had never visited? Conservatives argued that the silence of the Bible meant prohibition, while advocates argued it meant permission.

A compromise plan for cooperation among congregations for missions, the Louisville Plan, was proposed in 1868, but failed after a few years. Eventually most preachers and papers in the North, including the influential *Christian Standard*, supported the Missionary Society and other organizations for benevolent and

103

Caroline Neville Pearre

Sarah Lou Bostick

mission work. Those in the South generally opposed any organization beyond the local congregation.

After the Civil War, however, very important developments
emerged that expanded the work of societies considerably among
Disciples. Caroline Neville Pearre (pronounced Pa-ree) began a
work in 1874 that inspired several generations of Disciples. Her
inspiration came from a variety of locations. The ACMS had dis-
continued its foreign missions in Liberia, Jerusalem, and Jamaica.
Financial support for mission work dwindled, and while women in
other denominations were deeply committed to mission, among
Disciples no organized work for women existed.

On April 10, while engaged in her daily devotional, Caroline
Pearre decided to take action. She began calling together her
acquaintances and friends to do the organizational work for what
would become the Christian Woman's Board of Missions (CWBM).
By the time approximately seventy-five women from nine states
gathered in the basement of Richmond Street Christian Church in
Cincinnati on October 21, 1874 to form a national work, most of
them had already begun to gather commitments to this new effort
within their home churches.

Approved immediately by the General Missionary Convention
in Cincinnati, the CWBM raised funds to return missionaries to
Jamaica. Fifteen months later, Dr. William H. Williams and his family
left New York to plant new congregations in Jamaica. At the same

convention in 1874, the men met to talk about forming an additional mission society to concentrate solely on foreign missions. During the General Convention in Louisville the next year, they founded the Foreign Christian Missionary Society (FCMS). Eventually, the FCMS sent missionaries to England, Africa, and Tibet.

The women began to publicize their work with considerable success. They possessed a strong network of women throughout the country if only they could reach them with a mission message. Marcia M. B. Goodwin, publisher of *The Christian Monitor*, brought journalistic flair to the CWBM and volunteered several pages of her monthly women's magazine. By 1883, the CWBM began publishing *The Missionary Tidings*, which by 1919 reached more than sixty thousand subscribers. By the end of the century, the CWBM had become well-established and, by contemporary standards, fairly well-fixed financially as it approached assets nearing 1.5 million dollars.

The work of the CWBM enabled new connections between Disciples and ethnic communities, and particularly encouraged partnerships between white and black women near the turn of the century. In 1900 the ACMS turned over all its work among blacks to the CWBM. The CWBM had already become involved in supporting the work of the Southern Christian Institute, in Edwards, Mississippi, to provide education for African Americans. One of its graduates, Sarah Lou Bostick (1868-1948) became instrumental

Students and faculty of the Southern Christian Institute

105

in organizing African American women in Disciples churches. Led by her efforts, black women founded the Negro Christian Woman's Board of Mission. Under Bostick, its board cooperated with the CWBM board to create Jarvis Christian College, an important center of education in Texas for African Americans.

The CWBM also organized the first Disciples efforts to work among the Latino/Latina populations. In addition to mission work in Puerto Rico, Argentina, and Mexico, the CWBM created several home mission stations to serve these communities along the Texas and Mexico border. One of these, the Inman Christian Center, continues to serve as an important educational and health center for low income families in San Antonio.

The CWBM aided international connections as well. In 1887, an Ontario Christian Woman's Board of Missions developed in Canada and began recruitment of missionaries. Ontario supplied important leaders in missions for Disciples. Susie Rijnhart-Moyes (1868-1908) used her medical degree to serve in Tibet. Jessie Trout (1882-1956) became a missionary to Japan and, later, helped develop the Christian Women's Fellowship. By 1913, the CWBM revised its constitution to include on an equal basis the activities based in Canadian provinces. More than thirty-five Canadian women and men served in leadership roles in mission among Disciples during the early years, including Archibald McLean (1849-1920), the distinguished long-time president of the FCMS,

Jessie Trout

Archibald McLean

106

and Dr. Charles T. Paul (1869-1941), the first president of the College of Missions. The CWBM founded the college, with its first classes in the fall of 1910, as a nonsectarian graduate school to educate missionaries. The college demonstrated in pragmatic ways the central commitment of CWBM to the unity of the church.

As a result of efforts like the CWBM, and also the work of many Disciples women in temperance efforts, many men among Disciples began to encourage and support larger roles for women both in society and the church. Women began being recognized for their missionary service, and many of these women were ordained by congregations for that work. It is hard to determine who the first women ordained for these purposes were. Mention of women being ordained for these purposes are found as early as 1867. By 1888, ordinations to the preaching ministry begin to appear, with Clara Hale Babcock (1850-1925) being credited as the first. She was followed in short order by Jessie Coleman Monser, Sadie McCoy Crank (1863-1948), Bertha Mason Fuller, and Clara Espy Hazelrigg. Most of these women were very active in both the CWBM and the Women's Christian Temperance Union (WCTU).

There is little doubt that this increasing and visible role for women, both as missionaries sponsored by the societies and as preachers becoming pastors in congregations, increased the tension between more conservative and more progressive Disciples. Between 1891 and 1893, some twenty-nine different authors argued in the pages of *The Christian Standard* about the role of women in the church, and the proper interpretation of the Bible in relation to it.

INSTRUMENTAL MUSIC IN WORSHIP

Disciples were not the first to discuss the propriety of instrumental music in worship. Zwingli and Calvin had opposed the practice during the Reformation. In America, Congregational churches did not use instruments in worship until after the Revolutionary War. The issue did not appear in the early history of Disciples, perhaps because few frontier churches could afford instruments. The first recorded instance of an instrument used in worship among Disciples mentions the congregation in Midway, Kentucky in 1859. The minister, L. L. Pinkerton (1812-1875), brought in a melodeon to improve singing that, in his view, "scared even the rats from worship."

Only after the Civil War did many churches bring in instruments. Those who did argued that they were aids to singing and appealed to a new generation of worshippers. Opposition to instruments came primarily, but not exclusively, from the South. How could Northern churches waste money on organs while their Southern brothers and sisters starved? Others argued that the use of instruments put too much emphasis on the beauty of the music to the neglect of glorifying God. Their use did not promote "spiritual" worship.

As with the Missionary Society, many objected to instrumental music in worship because the Bible did not mention it. Since the New Testament mentioned singing but not instruments in worship, instruments were prohibited. On the other hand, those who supported their use argued that silence permitted instruments as an aid to singing just as silence permitted song books, song leaders, and church buildings as aids to worship. Interestingly, some applied the argument from silence differently to the issues. Thus, prominent leaders such as J. W. McGarvey (1829-1911) and Moses Lard supported the Missionary Society, but opposed instruments in worship.

Why did instrumental music get so much attention in the division? Perhaps because of its visibility. One could worship for years with a congregation and not know which members disagreed with your position on Missionary Societies and other issues. One could see immediately on entering a church building whether or not that congregation used instrumental music. But, perhaps more importantly, the issue became significant because it connected so easily with the sectional, economic, and urban cultural divides that had so dramatically affected the Disciples.

Although many leaders tried for a while to avoid making the instrument a matter of fellowship, it soon became one. After all, what could those conscientiously opposed to instruments do when a home congregation introduced one? Most thought they had little choice but to form a separate congregation, simpler and less ostentatious.

Steps Toward Division

Other divisive issues were discussed during this time, such as who should be allowed to partake of communion and the role of ministers. Was ministry a fulltime vocation where ministers settled in one location? Ministers, especially in the cities, expected a living

108

wage; those in rural locations often received their payment "in kind" and worked in another vocation to make ends meet. In spite of these so-called doctrinal disagreements and the existing cultural divide emerging among Disciples, an uneasy unity existed through the 1870s. By the 1880s, however, some were calling for recognition of a division they claimed had already occurred.

Chief among those was Daniel Sommer (1850-1940), who had followed Benjamin Franklin as editor of the *American Christian Review*. Sommer saw the changes among the churches during the previous thirty years as examples of apostasy. He made a distinction between "the Church of Christ" and the "so-called Christian Church." In August 1889, Peter Warren, an elder at Sand Creek, Illinois, read Sommer's "An Address and Declaration" (apparently a play on Thomas Campbell's *Declaration and Address*) to a large audience attending an annual encampment at Sand Creek, outlining his plan to save the movement from "innovations and corruptions." If leaders and churches would not give up practices such as instrumental music, support of the Missionary Society, located preachers, and others, then Sommer said "we cannot and will not regard them as brethren."

Most leaders in both the North and the South were not as quick as Sommer to proclaim a division. Eventually, though, they had to admit it. For many years, David Lipscomb tried not to acknowledge the division. By 1904, however, he had compiled a list of faithful churches and preachers, another way that a congregational movement identifies a split. When asked by the Director of the United States census if he should list Churches of Christ separately from Disciples of Christ in the 1906 religious census, Lipscomb painfully agreed that they were now two distinct bodies.

UNITY OR DIVISION?

Certainly the story of this and subsequent divisions are among the most embarrassing parts of Disciples heritage. How could a group that began as a unity movement later fracture and splinter? How could significant differences between the Stone and Campbell groups be overcome for the sake of unity in 1832, while seemingly less important issues divided those who followed by 1906?

T. B. Larimore

At least part of the answer to those questions lies in attitude. Most of these Christians believed it important to uphold certain ways of life in order to be faithful to God. And most were not shy about proclaiming them. The New Testament sets forth various standards of belief and practice. But the heart of the gospel found there always centers on Christ. The issues that generally divided Disciples did not. How can that be? Because Disciples, like most other Christians, often make minor issues or differences much more important and divisive than they should be.

Even in the decades following the Civil War some refused to split with their brothers and sisters over the issues and the ill feelings caused by the war. One such man was T. B. Larimore (1843-1929). Born in poverty in east Tennessee, Larimore sought baptism in Kentucky in 1864 and later attended Franklin College near Nashville, studying under Tolbert Fanning. Larimore spent the rest of his life as an educator and traveling evangelist, operating Mars Hill Academy near Florence, Alabama from 1871 to 1887.

A loyal son of the South, and influenced by some of the strongest opponents of the Missionary Society and instrumental music in worship, Larimore never supported either practice. Yet he refused to declare himself publicly on these issues because he believed the body of Christ should not divide over such matters. He saw his duty as a Christian evangelist to proclaim the good news of the New Testament. He had nothing to do with those questions over which "the wisest and best of men disagreed."

Larimore baptized over 10,000 people in his lifetime. But both sides continually pressured him to declare his position on the issues. Exasperated by the fact that he would not line up with either side, partisans criticized him harshly. But Larimore argued the importance of allowing freedom in matters of opinion. In this regard, Larimore reflected the heritage of Thomas Campbell and the *Declaration and Address*. When Campbell spoke of "being silent where the Bible is silent," he allowed for strong opinions on what that silence meant. Some might think silence permits; others might be sure it forbids. The "silence" Campbell called for refused to make those opinions divisive matters of faith.

Many in the Disciples at the end of the century turned Campbell's teaching upside down, insisting that "being silent" meant prohibiting any practice not mentioned in the New Testament. They even went farther and broke fellowship with those who approved of those practices. Larimore refused to do that. He would not break relations with those who were (in his opinion) wrong on the issues.

Larimore's fellowship with both groups existed in deed, not just in word. He continued to preach when invited, and was on the List of Preachers in the Disciples Yearbook until 1925. He wrote for religious papers in both groups. He spoke well of all. In his words: "I never call Christians or others 'anti's,' 'digressives,' 'mossbacks,' 'tackies,' or 'trash.' I concede to all, and accord to all, the same sincerity and courtesy I claim for myself, as the Golden Rule demands . . ."

Some in his day and in ours would say that such an attitude would lead the church into wholesale false teaching. Instead, if everyone in Larimore's day had imitated his attitude, perhaps the "issues" would never have divided Disciples. Larimore possessed an unusual awareness that Christian faith and an experience of God in Christ might somehow be able to transcend its connections to any variety of sectional, economic, agricultural, or urban circumstances. In any age, it seems like a good idea to follow the Golden Rule, to think the best of fellow Christians, to worship more and dispute less. That is the legacy of Larimore.

For Further Reading

Burnley, Lawrence A.Q. *The Cost of Unity: African-American Agency and Education in the Christian Church, 1865-1914*. Macon, Ga.: Mercer University Press, 2009.

Craddock, Fran, Martha Faw, and Nancy Heimer. *In the Fullness of Time: A History of Women in the Christian Church (Disciples of Christ)*. St. Louis: Chalice Press, 1999.

Foster, Douglas A. *Will the Cycle Be Unbroken? Churches of Christ Face the 21st Century*. Abilene: Abilene Christian University Press, 1994. See pages 147-159.

Garrett, Leroy. *The Stone-Campbell Movement*. Joplin, Mo.: College Press, 1994. See pages 381-405.

Harrell, David Edwin. *Sources of Division in the Disciples of Christ, 1865-1900*. Tuscaloosa: University of Alabama Press, 2003.

McAllister, Lester G. and Tucker, William E. *Journey in Faith*. St. Louis: Chalice Press, 1975. See pages 233-254.

Webb, Henry E. *In Search of Christian Unity*. 1990; new edition, Abilene: Abilene Christian University Press, 2003. See pages 201-227.

Questions for Discussion

1. How did post-Civil War conditions affect the discussion over missionary societies and instrumental music? Are there ever any "pure" discussions of doctrinal issues or do cultural circumstances always color our thinking?

2. How did women provide leadership during this crucial period of Disciples life?

3. How did the Disciples' notion of mission expand during these years?

4. Would following the Golden Rule help our relations with those with whom we differ in matters of faith?

THE INFLUENCES OF CULTURE

The twentieth century opened in the midst of considerable social distress. With its forays in the Spanish-American War of 1898, America had joined the ranks of world colonial powers. During this conflict, church and government leaders began to define America's mission in the world in global terms. America, they contended, would defend democracy across the globe and bring Western civilization and Christian morality to all peoples of the world. Leadership on the world's stage increased American vulnerability at home. Yet Americans seemed eager for the responsibility, unable at this early stage to understand the costs that might be associated with it. By the time of the sinking of the *Lusitania* on May 7, 1915, many Christians in America, most Disciples among them, called for American involvement in the crusade to defeat "evil" Germany.

Meanwhile, American cities grew rapidly (for example, Chicago grew from around 300,000 inhabitants to 1.7 million between 1870 and 1900) and economic distress accompanied the growth, increasing the chasm between rich and poor in the country. As many Americans prospered, and countless others lived in poverty, a new gulf opened among Christians as they tried to make sense of these realities. Some argued, especially after the war, that God blessed America and its citizens with wealth. When the war ended, American influence, these Christians argued, could open new mission fields. Christian wealth could be used to spread the gospel and lead to successful worldwide evangelization "in this generation." To be American meant to be favored by God. Poverty in such a great country could only result from sin and sloth.

113

Other Christians responded differently. Sole concern for individual salvation seemed woefully inadequate in light of the human suffering so evident in most of America's developing cities. The church needed to practice a "social gospel," one that addressed the sin found in social systems and tended to the material needs of the poor. For conservative Christians, these activities seemed more social, and thereby secular, than they were gospel. The gap between Christians continued to grow.

Christianity found itself challenged in a variety of areas in the late nineteenth century. New academic disciplines, like psychology and sociology, began to ask critically how religion and its ideas might be connected to the human mind or the human social context. Another new academic discipline specialized in the study of comparative religion. What did Christianity borrow from its cultural surroundings and from other religions? How did Christian theology develop over time, and how did its development mirror that of other religions?

Science also gained a new prominence in American culture when Charles Darwin set forth his evolutionary hypothesis in 1859, and others spent the remaining decades of the century exploring its connection to society and religion. The last quarter of the century also witnessed the explosion of technology: the development of such things as the telephone, four-stroke internal combustion engines and automobiles, phonographs and moving pictures, steam turbines, and very practical items like toilet paper, zippers, and long-lasting electric light bulbs. The world changed rapidly and some felt that Christian theology needed to change right along with it.

CULTURE OFFERS DISCIPLES A NEW DEFINITION OF UNITY

Beginning in the 1890s, Disciples leaders began to develop a revised notion of Christian unity. As the new definition gained currency, those with more traditional understandings of Christian unity refuted it, believing that it threatened the very identity of Disciples life. The new definition of unity grew in the soil of cultural assumptions which, ironically for Disciples, included a fear of diversity that often expressed itself in anti-Catholicism, racism, prejudice against non-Christian religions, nativistic anti-immigrant sentiments, and a cultural belief in unity and social coherence as if these were goods in themselves, regardless of the methods used to achieve them. These cultural assumptions were bolstered by a century of massive territorial expansion in the United States and nearly unlimited immigration throughout most of the nineteenth century. Events in the 1890s brought these prejudices to the surface in new ways, and most Disciples editors embraced these social tendencies.

Several factors contributed to the trend toward a stronger embrace of social unity. One of the more significant events occurred in 1893, the World's Columbian Exposition, or World's Fair, celebrating the 400th anniversary of the discovery of North America by Columbus. Held in Chicago from May 1 to October 31, the fair held great significance for most Disciples editors.

THE WORLD'S COLUMBIAN EXPOSITION, 1893

The World's Fair profoundly affected American culture. It gave birth to the Pledge of Allegiance, the Columbus Day holiday, and the Ferris Wheel. It introduced Americans to the electric light bulb, carbonated soda, the hamburger, Cracker Jacks, Cream of Wheat, Shredded Wheat, Aunt Jemima Syrup, Juicy Fruit Gum, picture postcards, and Pabst Beer, which, by the way, won a Blue Ribbon at the fair, hence: Pabst Blue Ribbon Beer. A children's writer, L. Frank Baum, visited the fair, and afterwards, created Oz. The midway of the fair, and Buffalo Bill's Wild West Show, inspired both Coney Island and Disneyland. The fair celebrated commerce and technology, and made both synonymous with progress.

The fair's basic message rebounded through the Disciples journals. James H. Garrison, for example, celebrated technology as synonymous with human progress, and tended to equate both of these with the activity of God in the world. He told his readers that "all these wonderful improvements are the highway [God] is building along which redeemed and crowned

James H. Garrison

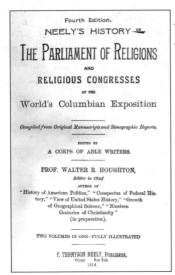

Fourth Edition.

NEELY'S HISTORY of

THE PARLIAMENT OF RELIGIONS

AND

RELIGIOUS CONGRESSES

AT THE

World's Columbian Exposition

Compiled from Original Manuscripts and Stenographic Reports.

EDITED BY

A CORPS OF ABLE WRITERS.

PROF. WALTER R. HOUGHTON,

Editor in Chief

AUTHOR OF

"History of American Politics," "Conspectus of Federal History," "View of United States History," "Growth of Geographical Science," "Nineteen Centuries of Christianity" (in preparation).

TWO VOLUMES IN ONE—FULLY ILLUSTRATED

F. TENNYSON NEELY, PUBLISHER,
Chicago   New York
1894

World's Parliament of Religion

humanity is to march to the City of God." Garrison repeated the fair's message concerning unity. "One of the most vivid impressions made upon us, as we looked upon this mingling of nationalities in friendly rivalry, was that of the growing unity of the race—the dawning consciousness of brotherhood." For moderate to progressive Disciples, the fair broadened the way they thought about unity. In addition to their emphasis on the unity of the church, they began to talk about the "unity of the race."

The World's Parliament of Religion (WPR), held at the World's Fair, also captured Disciples attention. Christians delivered most of the addresses (152 of 194). But other religions made presentations, including Buddhism, Judaism, Hinduism, Islam, Parsis, Shintoism, Confucianism, Taoism, and Jainism. Though the WPR intended to promote better understanding among the major religions of the world, its method seemed intent on other purposes. Christians took the lead and most of them took the superiority of Christianity for granted.

Christian participants in the WPR, and those who followed it in the news, became optimistic about social unity. Yet, they assumed that unity would result when the world's religions recognized that their truths are more profoundly present in Christianity. The diversity of Christian witness at the WPR also impressed Disciples leaders. Philip Schaff, in his address, argued for a form of Christian unity that would enable both unity and independence to coexist. Both the Federal Council of Churches of Christ in America (1908) and the first international missionary conference in Edinburgh (1910) would, within two decades, emerge from this kind of vision.

Along with other denominations meeting at the WPR, Disciples held their own congress in Chicago on September 13-14, 1893. Disciples delivered eight addresses during their congress, including two on the topic of Christian union written by F. D. Powers and

B. B. Tyler, both of whom were also regularly associated with the *Christian Standard*. Tyler's address, "The Promise of Christian Union in the Signs of the Times," presented his belief that secular affairs and tendencies all pointed in the direction of union. Tyler, like most of the Disciples leaders during this time, developed considerable optimism that all the signs associated with technology, progress, and civilization, so powerfully in evidence during the World's Fair, pointed in the direction of real union across both Christianity and the world.

THE SPANISH AMERICAN WAR, 1898

The Spanish-American War of 1898 became another cultural event that created considerable excitement in Disciples circles. Throughout the war, Disciples journals praised Commodore Dewey and his naval exploits. The *Christian Evangelist* even honored him with a cover. The *Gospel Advocate* was, of course, the exception. The *Advocate*, following the leadership of David Lipscomb, preached pacifism and conscientious objection to participation in the war. J. D. Tant reminded readers of the *Advocate* that "there can be Christians in Spain as well as in America, and those people are your brethren." He urged Christians not to become murderers for the sake of the country.

The war linked easily to the Christian optimism circulating among Disciples. All signs seemed to indicate that God intended history to march toward the kingdom of God. Garrison offered a good Disciples example of this belief when he proclaimed in 1891, "our Christian civilization" inexorably moves forward "toward perfection." God will reward all those who work toward this end. Garrison understood progress as synonymous with Christian civilization. "The pessimist," he exclaimed, has "no rightful place in the Christian Church." Looking ahead, Garrison prophesied, "Judging from present tendencies, and from what has been accomplished in the last decade, we may reasonably hope to see wonderful advancement in all the great departments of human life." Looking toward the twentieth century, Disciples leaders seemed to be losing their sense of the potential of human sin. They could not have imagined a holocaust or the devastation caused by atomic bombs.

Garrison also understood unity as a sign of progress: the union of citizens to purify politics and the union of Protestants to care for the poor and evangelize the "heathen" world. He expressed confidence that the unity of Christians would bring a positive "moral effect on the world" that will weaken general "infidelity." This belief in progress, and its optimistic connection to unity—always a Protestant (as opposed to Christian) unity—joined the chorus of cultural moralizing during the Spanish-American war.

ANGLO-SAXON ASSUMPTIONS, PROTESTANTS, AND RACISM

During the war, Disciples and others believed the progress of civilization depended entirely on the efforts of both Anglo-Saxons and Protestants. For these Protestants, a war against Spain meant a war against Catholicism. The events of 1898 brought out all the natural Protestant tendencies to express anti-Catholic views. The victory in this war, claimed the *Christian Standard*, "is the victory of Protestantism." And the "government of the United States is the richest gift of Protestantism to the world." Protestants had always tended to claim a kind of ownership of culture in the United States. But Disciples editors took these claims one step further. The spirit of true Protestantism, they wrote, resided best in the Disciples of Christ in North America; they are the "Standard-Bearers of Protestantism." With no hesitancy whatsoever, they could describe an alliance between Catholic priests and Satan to keep human beings away from the truth of Protestantism. These kinds of generalizations about Catholicism appeared everywhere in Disciples literature at the turn of the century.

In this war, Protestants also exhibited virulent forms of racism. Notions of unity formed around race and ethnic identification. A new stress fell on Anglo-Saxon Protestant unity. Though not an excuse, Disciples racism certainly embodied the cultural racism found almost everywhere in 1890. Like others, Disciples espoused the belief that all immigrant cultures must simmer in the great "melting pot" of American ideals. When the simmering ended, all would affirm American values, or as Disciples preferred to state it, Protestant values. Genuine citizenship meant the abandonment of any remnants of "foreign" heritage and the affirmation of Protestant

Anglo-Saxon values. The shorthand version often demanded that everyone had to at least act as if they were "white."

This spirit guided Disciples' relationship to both Native Americans or "Indians" and African-Americans or "Negroes" at the turn of the century. The journals commonly described the "Indian problem" and the "Negro problem." The solution to these problems would come once both groups were civilized and "Americanized." For example, Disciples editors promoted residential schools for Native American children. When children are separated from their tribes, they lose their bond with the past and are more quickly assimilated into civilized life. After "one or two generations," wrote editors at the *Christian Evangelist* in 1901, "the savage Indian . . . will have become a thing of the past and the Indian problem will be solved."

The government obliged. The Bureau for Indian Affairs forced Indian families onto farms and required their children to attend residential schools which prohibited the use of native languages and the study of Native American culture. The parents worked the farms and missed their children. During a drought, the Native Americans began to starve. In response, the government cut rations in half. The Ghost Dance gained popularity among the natives, which frightened authorities and eventually led to a bloody massacre of more than 153 Lakota Sioux. When editors at the *Christian Evangelist* finally heard of the massacre, they reported that "the Indian outbreak now happily about terminated, will bring about a thorough examination of [government] management, and possibly a change of methods."

Earlier in the nineteenth century, Disciples established a "Board of Negro Evangelization and Education." Most Disciples agreed when the *Christian Evangelist* reported in 1893 that "no duty whatsoever should rest with greater weight on our consciences than that of coming to the rescue of this people with the power of education and the gospel to enlighten, to save and elevate them." Disciples, like others, believed education would solve the "Negro problem." Such attitudes naturally ignored the roles played by social systems or racism. To curb the primitive social skills and lawlessness associated with blacks, solutions had to involve either education or white social power, or both. An editorial in the *Christian Oracle* in 1891 suggested that "material development in the South," accompanied by "Yankee"

119

immigration to the South, would eventually solve the "Negro problem." When whites clearly outnumbered the blacks, they could freely
grant "rights so soon as they know in so doing they are not imperiling
their own." This kind of condescension marks most Disciples discussions during these years, even among the most progressive social
gospel advocates.

The very fact that Disciples editors decided that the new century demanded a new name for the *Christian Oracle* illustrates an
unbridled optimism. "Optimism," wrote Charles Clayton Morrison
(1874-1966), the *Christian Century* editor, "is the spirit of the glo-
rious Gospel." This new century would be the "Christian century."
The editor at the *Century* could wax eloquent about the "unity of
the race—yea, the unity of all life, even the unity of the universe."
He spoke of the way God uses the secular realities of the cities, science and technology, history, psychology, and even modern war
like the one just past to bring about unity in everything. Those things
standing against this kind of unity (Catholics, immigrants, Indians,
blacks, Spaniards, Filipinos, saloons, etc.) must be civilized,
"Americanized," or "Protestantized" into unity. For some Disciples,
unity lost an explicit and unique theological connection to the body
of Christ and became increasingly connected to concepts like progress, civilization, Americanization, and becoming Protestant.

These cultural assumptions included the belief that great civi-
lizations and their political leadership always had to be "manly"
and represent the best aspects of human character, which were
best represented in white men. In the late 1890s, America could
not back down from a challenge without seriously threatening
both its manhood and its own sense of racial superiority. Disciples
were as wrapped up in this mentality as any other group of
American citizens.

Disciples theology written in the nineteenth century is largely
white, middle class, and male. Disciples women labored in the
church, even built organizations, but struggled against great odds
to gain access to higher education, theological education, and leadership in the church. African Americans, members of Disciples
congregations from near the beginning, struggled to find a voice
and a meaningful place in shaping the church. Preston Taylor
(1849-1931) became an influential figure in the African American
search for ministry and leadership among Disciples.

120

After service in the Civil War, and success in constructing railroads, Taylor founded a funeral home in Nashville. Since his days as an elder in a black Christian church at the age of twenty (1869), however, Taylor practiced ministry among Disciples. He worked hard to help black Disciples shape their own destiny and church life. He led the effort to form the National Christian Missionary Convention (1917). He believed organized work among blacks became necessary because "the attitude of our white brotherhood on the race question accounts largely for our smallness." In his inaugural address to the convention, which he served with distinction as president for fourteen years, Taylor claimed, "The Disciples of Christ, strange as it may seem, need the colored people . . . For if the white brother can include in his religious theory and practice the colored people as real brothers, he will have avoided the heresy of all heresies."

Preston Taylor

OTHER CULTURAL THEMES ALSO CHALLENGED DISCIPLES

Disciples reflected a struggle with cultural themes in a number of other areas during these years, particularly temperance, women's suffrage, urbanization and issues related to labor, and the desire to develop a greater education system among Disciples. These concerns also connected to the themes of unity, progress and technology, Christianization, civilization, and Americanization emerging from the World's Fair and the Spanish-American War.

The relationship between faith and culture is rarely a simple one. The Disciples captivation with cultural themes, while harmful in many respects, did yield some benefit. Over time, many of those concerns, in fact, created in Disciples a new awareness of the connection between the gospel and social justice. This awareness, in turn, helped them to uncover and begin to address their own racism and their participation in other equally unchristian cultural assumptions. These attitudes began to change as Disciples became more thoroughly involved in global mission. By the end of the 1950s, Disciples, as a movement, finally experienced some success in challenging the cultural assumptions concerning race, Catholics, progress, and civilization that they had held for most of the past century. In fact, the early years of the twentieth century had a profound impact on the theological development of Disciples. Ministers entertained a new approach to the Bible and ultimately to the church and its mission.

For Further Reading

Addresses Delivered at the World's Congress and General Missionary Conventions of the Church of Christ Held at Chicago, in September, 1893. Chicago: S. J. Clarke, 1893.

Bederman, Gail. *Manliness & Civilization: A Cultural History of Gender and Race in the United States, 1880-1917.* Chicago: University of Chicago Press, 1995.

Burnley, Lawrence A. Q. *The Cost of Unity: African-American Agency and Education in the Christian Church, 1865-1914.* Macon, Ga.: Mercer University Press, 2009.

Burris, John P. *Exhibiting Religion: Colonialism and Spectacle at International Expositions, 1851-1893.* Charlottesville: University Press of Virginia, 2001.

Clymer, Kenton J. *Protestant Missionaries in the Philippines, 1898-1916: An Inquiry into the American Colonial Mentality.* Champaign: University of Illinois Press, 1986.

Haddad, Yvonne Yazbeck, Jane I. Smith, and John L. Esposito. *Religion and Immigration: Christian, Jewish and Muslim Experiences in the United States.* Lanham, Md.: Rowman & Littlefield, 2003.

Higham, John. *Strangers in the Land: Patterns of American Nativism, 1860-1925.* New Brunswick, N.J.: Rutgers University Press, 1988.

Hoganson, Kristin L. *Fighting for American Manhood: How Gender Politics Provoked the Spanish-American and Philippine-American Wars.* New Haven: Yale University Press, 1998.

Hopkins, Dwight. *Down, Up, and Over: Slave Religion and Black Theology.* Philadelphia: Fortress Press, 2000.

Jha, Sandhya. *Room at the Table: Struggle for Unity and Equality in Disciples History*. St. Louis: Chalice Press, 2009. See pages 16-27.

Lyda, Hap. "A History of Black Christian Churches (Disciples of Christ) in the United States Through 1899." Ph.D. diss., Vanderbilt University, 1972.

Machado, Daisy L. *Of Borders and Margins: Hispanic Disciples in Texas, 1888-1945*. New York: Oxford University Press, 2003.

QUESTIONS FOR DISCUSSION

1. How did the Disciples notion of Christian unity change to reflect the cultural ethos in the United States during the late-nineteenth century?

2. How did cultural assumptions about race, religion, and gender affect the Disciples understanding of their relationship to ethnic groups, immigrants, Native Americans, Roman Catholics, women, and even war?

3. This chapter examines how culture affected Disciples thinking in the late nineteenth century. In what ways do you think culture affects Christian thinking today? Can you name more recent examples where Christians may be confusing cultural assumptions with the gospel?

A NEW THEOLOGY

Perhaps the most important change affecting theology at the end of the nineteenth century resulted from new approaches to studying the Bible that appeared first in Germany. First known as advocates of "higher criticism," these historical biblical critics began to look beyond the literary characteristics or precise wording of the original text (so-called "lower criticism") to examine its historical and social background and sources as well as a variety of questions related to its date and authorship. These new approaches challenged traditional assumptions, such as who wrote various Old and New Testament books. The conclusions of these new biblical critics even challenged the historical reliability of the Gospels, Matthew, Mark, Luke, and John. Historical criticism also made connections between culture and context in order to show how these influenced the content of the biblical text itself.

Some Disciples attacked these new forms of understanding the Bible, particularly John W. McGarvey (1829-1911) who was long associated with the College of the Bible in Lexington, Kentucky. He espoused the traditional Disciples perspective that the Bible contained universally binding rules that govern the lives of all Christians in all times. Meanwhile Alexander Proctor (1825-1900), James H. Garrison (1842-1931), and Isaac Errett (1820-1888) represented a more moderate approach. They had not bought all the assumptions of the biblical critics, but they believed, as Proctor put it, in an "insistence upon a free spirit of inquiry, the encouragement of new methods of biblical study, the idea that love is central to Christian theology and that God's power is manifested in Christ, the belief that God's creative methodology was evolutionary, and the fascination with science." At the Disciples convention in Indianapolis in 1897, Proctor and McGarvey stood on the platform together. They had been long-time friends, and Proctor had even officiated at McGarvey's wedding. But as they stood together in 1897, as Joseph Jeter put it in his study of Proctor, "one [was] looking to the future and its possibilities, the other recalling a past that was even then dying."

Increasing numbers of Disciples ministers received their education from places like Yale and Chicago. By 1920, some 153 ministers had completed their work in these two schools. In the next couple of decades, an additional 200 ministers graduated from these seminary programs, and many also sought doctoral degrees. Edwin Becker has shown that forty-eight Disciples had received Ph.D. degrees from either Chicago or Yale by 1940. The graduates of these ecumenical programs shared many characteristics. They found Christian faith completely compatible with scientific knowledge. They employed modern academic tools to understand faith. And they also believed Christ taught that God's love extended to all and included an emphasis on justice for all.

Liberalism among Protestants fell largely into two different camps during this period. Most Disciples leaders represented the milder brand of Protestant liberalism known as "Evangelical liberalism" or "Christocentric liberalism." They hoped to fit Christian theology to expressions required by modern life. If reason required a slight change in theological expression, these Christians were willing to adjust. Among evangelical liberals, the term "Back to Christ" was common, and thus fit naturally the interests of many Disciples ministers.

A much smaller number of Disciples fit into the more radical form of Protestant liberalism known as "modernistic liberalism" or "scientific modernism." For these Christians, science or modern philosophy became their sole authority. They understood religion primarily from the perspective of how it meets human need. Christianity, like all other religious faiths, arose to meet human psychological and sociological needs. Scientific modernism particularly flourished at the University of Chicago. Fundamentalism emerged as an organized movement in the early decades of the twentieth century in response to these kinds of developments in Christian theology. Disciples ministers could be found in each of these new categories of Christian theology.

Among Disciples, the most influential voice for scientific modernism belonged to Edward Scribner Ames (1870-1958) who served as professor of philosophy at the University of Chicago after he earned the first Ph.D. degree offered by the university's philosophy department in 1895. He had done his undergraduate work at Yale. In addition, Ames served as pastor of the Hyde Park Church (in later years known as the University Church) for forty years. As early as 1918, Ames represented the meaning of scientific modernism for Disciples in his book *The New Orthodoxy*. For his theological understanding, Ames drew from the natural and social sciences (including sociology and psychology) rather than from biblical sources.

Few Disciples advocated the form of humanism represented in Ames' thought. Yet his teaching and presence helped many Disciples overcome the style of fundamentalism that had become popular during the early part of the twentieth century in many corners of American Protestantism. However, many twentieth-century Disciples reflected some of the weaknesses associated with Ames's position. As Clark Williamson and Chuck Blaisdell have observed, Ames was unable to articulate any clear "norm of appropriateness" from within the Christian tradition. Christianity had nothing to offer that might "serve to govern or criticize proposed theories and practices." When Ames spoke of Christ, like most of liberal Protestantism in the early twentieth century, he basically described his own, and his culture's, values and moral beliefs. For Ames, the message of civilization and the message of the church at its best were indistinguishable from one another.

Not all Disciples at the University of Chicago were scientific modernists. Herbert L. Willett (1864-1944), the most well-known among Disciples liberals at Chicago, clearly represented evangelical liberal interests and concerns throughout his career. After an education at Bethany and four years serving as a pastor in Ohio, Willett attended Yale and then became the first Disciple to earn a Ph.D. in Semitics (the Semitic languages including Acadian, Aramaic,

Herbert L. Willett

and Hebrew) when he graduated from the University of Chicago in 1896. He accepted a faculty appointment but continued to serve as pastor for churches in Chicago throughout his career. Though Willett could not accurately be described as a radical biblical critic, he did become a controversial figure among Disciples in this period because he accepted some of the moderate conclusions associated with higher criticism.

In 1893, a conversation between Herbert Willett and W. D. MacClintock, a professor of English in the University of Chicago, led to a plan to create a Disciples Divinity House (DDH) at the university. In 1894, "the House" was officially chartered with Willett as its first dean. During the first three decades, DDH constituted more an association of Disciples students preparing for ministry at the university than an actual physical location. Eventually, in 1928, when E. S. Ames served as the Dean of DDH, "the House" dedicated its current building. The DDH, with substantial resources including both the building and a variety of endowments for scholarships and other purposes, has exercised significant influence among Disciples through its graduates. More than a physical location with resources, however, the DDH through the years has kept its primary ethos as an association of Disciples seeking to combine excellence in educational preparation with a concern for visionary leadership in both the church and the academy.

In 1903, Willett published *Basic Truths of the Christian Faith*, a book addressing theological themes that sought to reach a popular rather than scholarly audience. The book represents several clear shifts in Disciples theology occasioned by Disciples who adopted more liberal perspectives. Any notion of efforts to effect a contemporary restoration of the early church is gone. The traditional Disciples emphasis on the epistles and Acts is replaced by a serious engagement with the life of Christ as depicted in the gospels. "It must be remembered," Willett told his readers, "that the Gospels, containing as they do the teachings of our Lord, are the greatest of all documents for Christian culture." His primary focus is on the life and teachings of Christ, not on biblical texts for their own sake. The teachings of Christ are far more important for Willett than any church's declaration of Christ's divinity.

Willett located inspiration in the actual history of Israel and early Christians, rather than in words found in the Bible. The authority of the Bible is found more in what it enables than in what it is. For Willett, the Bible produces "a better order of living" and possesses the ability "to make clear the way of human fellowship with God." These qualities enabled by the narratives of scripture are far more important than any infallibility claimed for the text itself.

Willett's *Basic Truths* emphasized human initiative and participation in the kingdom of God. Baptism became "the public ceremony of allegiance by which the Christian knight takes upon himself the service of his Lord." Where Campbell stressed a kingdom largely moving toward us, Willett argued that God "has no other way of getting the kingdom organized in the world than by the ministries of his people." Instead of a literal second coming of Christ, Willett described a second coming that was "continuous and spiritual," found not in "a mechanical and material millennium," but rather in the advance of God's love among human beings. These themes produced a church more aware of the social problems of the time and fostered a renewed commitment to church unity. Yet it also led to a rather uncritical vision of history as progress that overconfidently predicted humanity's ability to accomplish great things in the name of God.

Ames and Willett were both founding members of the Campbell Institute. After several years of discussion, Disciples at Chicago founded the institute in 1896 "to encourage and keep alive a scholarly spirit and to enable its members to help each other to a riper scholarship by the free discussion of vital problems." For the most part, the institute represented values associated with liberalism and university-educated Disciples. It served to bolster the morale of liberal-leaning Disciples who hoped to change the conservative culture they felt characterized most of Disciples life. By 1903, the Institute had begun to publish its own journal, and its influence among Disciples, and the controversies that influence generated, had also begun to grow.

Ames edited the journal, renamed *The Scroll*, until 1908, when publication was suspended. *The Christian Standard*, which represented conservative Disciples concerns after Isaac Errett's death in 1888, regularly took editors at *The Scroll* to task for their liberal theology. This kind of negative attention led to the resignation of Alva Taylor from his pastorate in Eureka, Illinois, and also to conservative efforts to block Willett's invitation to speak at the centennial assembly in Pittsburgh in 1909. A few years after *The Scroll* resumed publication, Ames assumed the editor's chair again in 1925 and remained until 1951. By 1925, the main lines of Disciples life had become much more accommodating to the liberal ideas associated with the Institute.

Throughout the early decades of the twentieth century, however, the majority of Disciples congregations were likely closer to fundamentalism than they were to either evangelical liberalism or scientific modernism. Yet, the influence of the Disciples House, the Campbell Institute, and a new generation of Disciples leaders began to transform Disciples church culture. In 1945, a conservative critic noted that, "while only 6.42% of the denomination's ministers were members of the Campbell Institute, members held 37.5% of the offices in the International convention of Disciples of Christ, 75% of the offices in the Board of Higher Education, and 80% of the chief executive positions in cooperating institutions." These statistics demonstrate the growing influence among Disciples wielded by members of the Campbell Institute.

INITIATIVES IN CHRISTIAN UNITY

As seen in the last chapter, the Disciples began adopting a new notion of Christian unity by the end of the nineteenth century. Even though cultural optimism infected the Disciples understanding of unity, they continued to believe unity rested in one's relationship to Christ. In other words, unity belongs to the body of Christ. Human beings don't create it; it exists as a gift of God.

As Disciples entered the twentieth century, leaders began to think of Disciples as a denomination. For most of them, a sense of repentance accompanied the recognition. Being leaders in a denomination meant they participated in the division of the church. During the nineteenth century, Disciples insisted they were calling Christians out of the denominations. But now they began to recognize they were in one. In some ways, Disciples must have felt like Pogo when he looked around at the trash in Okefenoke Swamp and told Porky, "We have met the enemy and he is us."

As the twentieth century progressed, Disciples gradually became more self-aware. No longer could they claim their own theological development had been free of human error. They had made mistakes just like all the other churches. This led them to see just how much they needed the witness of other churches. Together, perhaps the churches could discover the depth of Christian faith and overcome their own particular shortcomings. In unity, they could express more completely what no one of the denominations alone could express.

With the advent of new approaches to the Bible, and a new emphasis on a critical analysis of their own history, Disciples became more aware of how difficult it is for human beings to understand and represent God's will with complete certainty. They experienced a new humility, and began to confront their own racism and prejudices. They expressed a greater degree of tolerance toward others. This enabled them to engage in efforts for visible Christian unity with a new energy and sense of purpose.

The word ecumenical comes from the Greek word *oikoumene*. The word actually means "the inhabited earth." For most of the twentieth century, the church has used it to describe efforts to unify Christian groups across the earth. The first organized expression of ecumenism in the United States arose when churches shared efforts to create the Federal Council of the Churches of Christ in America (FCC). The fact the Disciples joined these early efforts

J. Irwin Miller (front left) with President Lyndon B. Johnson

provided further testimony that Disciples were coming to understand themselves as an organized church instead of a movement. With this move, their leaders were actually joining an association of denominations. Most of the people in the pews did not pay much attention at the time, nor did most understand its significance.

Because of the movement's historical commitment to church unity, it made sense to join the ecumenical movement in its earliest national and international manifestations. Disciples continue to participate fully in all organized aspects of the movement. They have provided significant leadership in most of these circles. Mossie Wyker served as president of United Church Women—now known as Church Women United. Edgar DeWitt Jones served as president of the FCC and J. Irwin Miller served as president of the National Council of Churches (the modern version of the FCC). Three of the nine general secretaries (chief executives) in the sixty year history of the National Council of Churches have been Disciples: Roy G. Ross (1954-1963), Joan Brown Campbell, (1991-1999) and Michael Kinnamon (appointed in 2007).

Disciples engaged international ecumenical work from the beginning as well. They sent leaders to all the major international missionary conferences, beginning with Edinburgh in 1910, and all the meetings that followed including through mid-century the meetings in Jerusalem (1928), Madras, India (1938), Whitby, Canada (1947), and Willengen, Germany (1952). In 1948, Disciples

Peter Ainslie

Paul Crow, Jr.

also joined with others to form the World Council of Churches. Disciples have faithfully attended with full delegations, and responded in writing to most of its deliberations, those addressing both "Life and Work" and "Faith and Order." Conversations with others have deeply enriched the Disciples experience of Christian faith since 1900.

Historians identify 1910 as the year when ecumenism became a worldwide experience with the Edinburgh Missionary Conference. In the same year, Peter Ainslie, pastor of Christian Temple in Baltimore, led Disciples of Christ to create an organizational commitment to Christian unity, the Council on Christian Union (CCU). The office has served Disciples in all its ecumenical conversations since 1910. Through the twentieth century, the CCU carried on conversations with Presbyterians, Baptists, the United Church of Christ, and a variety of denominations associated with the Consultation on Church Union (COCU), a forty year discussion among nine denominations, and its later incarnation as Churches Uniting in Christ (CUIC). Now known as the Council on Christian Unity (since 1954), its leaders have come from the ranks of ministers committed to unity as an essential part of their ministerial calling. In 1999, Robert Welsh became president following Paul Crow, Jr., who led the council for twenty-five years.

CONCLUSION

By the end of the 1920s, Disciples had divided into at least three distinct forms of expressions. The strict restorationists read the Bible through literal eyes, expecting the church in all times to live precisely according to its precepts. They believed the perfect church to be static and conformed to forms deduced from the New Testament.

On the other end of the spectrum were those who relied primarily upon human experience and Christ's example as the primary authorities in Christian faith. They were progressives who argued that the goal of all Christianity was to make human life more successful. The conclusions of science were not to be feared but rather embraced. For some, like Edward Scribner Ames, science and the social sciences, more than Christian faith, constituted the starting point for all thinking about truth. Ames and the few Disciples who shared his view had a religious faith in science and the ability of human beings to reason their way to truth and God's kingdom.

In between these two views stood the territory occupied by most Disciples leaders during this period. Most of them represented a moderate form of restorationism. They weren't strict or legalistic in their reading of the Bible. They emphasized Christ, rather than a text, as the guiding spirit of the movement. They wanted to avoid "tests of fellowship" but also stressed the Disciples concern for a restored church, and called all other Christians to recognize the wisdom of their approach. They believed in the value of science and reason, but also affirmed the need for the church to look to the Bible for patterns to guide its life and expression. They worked conscientiously toward visible unity. This group believed in expediency and compromise, in the attempt to emphasize whatever unity could be claimed within diversity.

They were largely unaware of the way contemporary cultural assumptions guided their interpretation of faith. Most were dedicated to the institution of the church, trying desperately to hold everything together, to mediate compromises between the strict restorationist and the progressive wings of the Disciples movement. They tended to work pragmatically, to affirm both the autonomy of congregations and the democratic principle that affirmed the importance of the majority will for areas of church work represented in the general life of the church.

By 1900, Disciples leadership, and large numbers of their congregations, had entered the mainline of Protestantism. Disciples worked cooperatively with Methodists, Presbyterians, Baptists, and others on the mission field. Rather than trying to "capsize" these denominational groups, and make them "Christians only," Disciples took for granted their status as Christians and worked alongside them in numerous endeavors. These trends did not please all Disciples. Conservative Disciples still insisted on the need to call the denominations back to the simple gospel plea of Disciples tradition. By 1920, however, Disciples leaders were clearly set in their trajectory to join mainline Protestantism as full participants. As evangelical Protestantism divided into liberal and conservative streams during the first half of the century, Disciples paddled their boat toward the left fork.

For Further Reading

Ames, Edward Scribner. *The New Orthodoxy*. Chicago: University of Chicago, 1918.

Ames, Van Meter, ed. *Beyond Theology: The Autobiography of Edward Scribner Ames*. Chicago: University of Chicago Press, 1959.

Becker, Edwin L. *Yale Divinity School and the Disciples of Christ, 1872-1989*. Nashville: Disciples Historical Society, 1990.

Boring, M. Eugene. *Disciples and the Bible: A History of Disciples Biblical Interpretation in North America*. St. Louis: Chalice Press, 1997.

Jeter, Joseph R. *Alexander Proctor: The Sage of Independence*. Claremont, Ca.: Disciples Seminary Foundation, 1983.

Pearson, Samuel C. "The Campbell Institute: Herald of the Transformation of an American Religious Tradition." *The Scroll* (Spring 1978), 1-63.

Perdue, Leo G. "The Disciples and Higher Criticism: The Formation of an Intellectual Tradition." In D. Newell Williams, *A Case Study of Mainstream Protestantism: The Disciples Relation to American Culture, 1880-1989*. Grand Rapids: Eerdmans, 1991. See pages 71-106.

Willett, Herbert L. *Basic Truths of the Christian Faith*. Chicago: Christian Century Company, 1903.

Williamson, Clark M. and Charles R. Blaisdell, "Disciples and Mainstream Protestant Theology." In D. Newell Williams, *A Case Study of Mainstream Protestantism: The Disciples Relation to American Culture, 1880-1989*. Grand Rapids: Eerdmans, 1991. See pages 107-138.

Questions for Discussion

1. In the late nineteenth and early twentieth century, several new approaches to theology developed among Disciples. Can you describe them and what kinds of things contributed to their development?

2. What role did an increasing emphasis on education play during these years?

3. In what ways did Disciples create new relationships with other denominations in this period? What new kinds of ecumenical connections captured their attention?

4. What three theological groupings characterize Disciples during these years? Which one of the three seemed larger and more influential?

CHAPTER

A NEW STRUCTURE, NEW MISSION, AND NEW DIVISION

The nineteenth century had been one of rapid expansion for Disciples. At the turn of the century, the Disciples had more than 1,100,000 members. Between 1880 and 1896, membership had exploded from around 400,000 to over 1,000,000 members. For those sixteen years, the Disciples averaged approximately 37,500 new members a year. As their centennial celebration in Pittsburgh (1909) approached, Disciples had considerable optimism about the future.

Why had they grown so rapidly? Many said it was due to their emphasis on unity, their simple message that all Christians are one because of their affirmation that Christ is the "Son of God." But others recognized that cultural factors also played a role. One of their own, James A. Garfield, had been elected president in 1881. Though he was quickly assassinated, the president brought considerable attention to the Disciples. They had reached respectability in the culture. In short, Disciples had arrived and had integrated well into the leadership circles of the cities and rural communities throughout Missouri, Illinois, Indiana, Kentucky, Iowa, Ohio, and Tennessee. About 70% of the more than one million Disciples lived in those seven states.

Beginning with the loss of about 160,000 members who had formally connected with the Churches of Christ by 1906, the burgeoning growth began to slow considerably. Disciples kept at it, however. They produced a good number of well-known evangelists, including Charles Reign Scoville (1869-1937), Charles R. L. Vawter (1879-1935), and

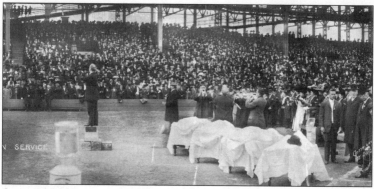

Centennial Celebration in Pittsburgh

Jesse M. Bader (1886-1963). But the days of rapid growth had gone. While they continued slow growth for the first half of the century, rapid decline would be the order of the day after the 1960s.

Disciples still found much to brag about in 1909. They had more than 11,000 congregations. They claimed twenty-seven colleges, "with property valued at four million dollars." The three missionary societies raised over one million dollars for mission in 1908 alone. A newly developed Board of Church Extension provided assistance to build houses of worship. More evidence of the strength of women's work among Disciples emerged when, in 1886, a number of women met to discuss forming an organization to aid women and children. By 1909, the resulting National Benevolent Association had already been at work for a dozen years, achieving substantial results among orphans, the aged, and the poor.

But for many, the lack of a more centralized approach to church life meant needless repetition and too much competition for money. The work of the three missionary societies seemed the most obvious example. The CWBM and the FCMS both had missionaries in Africa, India, and China. The CWBM and the ACMS were both operating in Canada and the United States. All three of the societies had their own boards, magazines, leadership, and congregational fund-raising mechanisms.

Disciples began to question the competitive spirit that seemed to accompany their loose-knit connections and congregational polity. Anybody with an idea could create an organization, pitch it to others, raise money, and describe it as Disciples related. At a meeting in Buffalo in 1906, leaders looked at alternatives. They hoped to create a delegate convention to replace mass meetings where everybody who showed up had a vote. That way, congregations could decide together who would legitimately represent Disciples across the world. Though accepted as part of a new constitution in Louisville in 1912, the idea of a delegate convention failed for lack of support elsewhere. By 1917, the convention meeting in Kansas City approved a revised constitution that solidified the mass meeting. But it also created a smaller, more representative and delegate-oriented Committee on Recommendations to screen all items before moving them to the mass assembly. Finally, the constitution provided a new name for the convention, the International Convention, because these meetings always included congregations from both the United States and Canada.

Given their experience with periodical wars, Disciples also sought to secure a publishing venue that could represent all Disciples. When Robert A. Long (1850-1934) bought out James H. Garrison's (1842-1931) controlling interest in the Christian Publishing Company, he placed it directly under the control of a board of trustees charged with running the company in the interest of Disciples. With this move, *The Christian Evangelist* became the Disciples official voice in 1909 in contrast to journals like *The Christian Standard*, which continued to remain in private hands.

While discussions around consolidation continued, the various agencies among Disciples united to raise money when they created the Men and Millions Movement of 1913. By 1919, the effort had raised nearly six million dollars to be spread across the various agencies. In 1917, a committee of leaders emerged to create a new united organization, one with equal representation of both men and women on its board. At the 1919 convention, meeting in Cincinnati, Disciples created the United Christian Missionary Society (UCMS). This new society combined the Foreign Christian Missionary Society, the American Christian Missionary Society, the

Men and Millions Movement of 1913

139

Christian Woman's Board of Mission, the Board of Church Extension, the National Benevolent Association, and the Board of Ministerial Relief.

The UCMS combined the most important areas of Disciples ministry. The society oversaw all mission work at home and abroad, benevolence work, the preparation of materials for religious education, congregational development, evangelism, provision of ministerial relief and pensions, and the recruitment of new ministers and missionaries. The governing board had a broad membership, half men and half women, representing all regions of the country where Disciples had meaningful presence. Within the completion of its first decade, the UCMS had over 340 missionaries in ten locations across the world. At home, the society created Bible chairs at several state universities, planted new churches, worked with Native Americans in Yakima, Washington, French Acadians in Louisiana, African Americans in the South, and immigrants on the eastern seaboard.

The UCMS accomplished significant work in its first decades, but the growing complexity of Disciples life soon created new concerns and tensions. Not the least of these tensions arose when the women, who contributed through the CWBM the lion's share of assets for the new society, discovered that the new society considerably diminished their ability to contribute as leaders. Promises to split leadership positions never actually materialized. Those who contributed as staff labored under an unfair salary structure that favored the men in their role as heads of households. In 1920, the

staff included sixteen men and nine women. By 1933, Disciples women at the time noted the disparity had grown to seventeen men and only four women. In a 1931 letter to Lela Taylor, who worked as an officer in the UCMS, Effie Cunningham expressed her heartfelt feelings on the matter: "One thing that cuts so deep is that in addition to all the burdens you have, our good and true women have the additional and unnecessary heartaches and handicaps of the injustice that has come to

Effie Cunningham

140

them. This hurts so because we who helped prepare for our United Society thought we had safeguarded the work and workers from this very thing."

In spite of these cultural and denominational prejudices, women made a considerable contribution throughout the twentieth century in mission circles. Anna Atwater, the first woman to be named vice-president of the UCMS (1920-1925), provided significant direction in shaping the missionary activities of the Disciples. Others, like Ora Leigh

Anna Atwater

Shepherd and Jessie M. Trout, provided strong leadership while many more women served on the mission field. Disciples women formed the International Christian Women's Fellowship, followed by the World Christian Women's Fellowship, the latter meeting in conjunction with the World Convention of the Churches of Christ.

For women, like men, ministry took a variety of forms. Rosa Page Welch (1900-1994) played a key role in the integration of Disciples' churches at mid-century as an African-American civil rights activist, singing artist, and educator. She had attended Southern Christian Institute where she discovered a love for music. After her graduation she led singing at "evangelistic meetings." From there white Disciples asked her to perform and lead singing at youth conferences and other meetings. At many of these events, she was the only non-white person but her efforts helped bring down racial barriers. In 1952, she traveled and sang throughout Africa, Asia, Europe, and South America. For two years in the early 1960s, she served as a missionary to Nigeria on behalf of the Church of the Brethren. She later worked with Disciples in the United Promotion Office in the general church.

The UCMS, Open Membership, and a New Division

There is little doubt that the UCMS and its history illustrates the most powerful aspect of Disciples church life for nearly fifty years (1919-1968). The power of editors began to wane with the turn of the century, and UCMS leaders filled the vacuum. Using the official publishing arm, they cranked out resources for congregations and interpreted all phases of Disciples work. The staff traveled the country speaking in congregations. Though some tried, most found it difficult to counter the UCMS's ability to speak for Disciples. No other body could effectively check its power. Most of its leaders exercised that power both responsibly and effectively. Their work enabled Disciples to make a contribution to Christian mission, ecumenical endeavors, and Christian education far beyond the strength of their numbers. Through the UCMS and its core of committed Christian leaders, Disciples presented a denominational face during the years when, in reality, they were simply a loose association of very diverse congregations.

In most of its work, the UCMS operated without careful attention to any particular theological understanding of mission. Leaders depended on ecumenical rationale for work in home and foreign fields. Even then, they tended to pick and choose rationale that fit with their immediate and practical needs. Disciples tended toward the pragmatic; if something worked, they usually deemed it appropriate. For example, few Disciples leaders at the time explored the important theological questions related to world mission. Might the incarnation of Christ and all that it means express a theological truth that the "Word" of God may be active across the world in ways Christians in the West might not recognize? Disciples were too busy involved in mission work to engage theological questions like these very carefully.

Early in the history of the UCMS, a controversy erupted that illustrates the Disciples' inability to deal adequately with theological issues. When rumors surfaced that Disciples missionaries might be practicing open membership on the mission field, many Disciples vigorously protested. The ensuing controversy affected Disciples life for decades.

The controversy did not begin on the mission field. Open membership, the practice of accepting adults into congregational membership who had not been immersed, had been an issue since the early days of the movement. In the 1870s, W. T. Moore became minister of a congregation in London known for the practice. Some congregations closer to home also began to practice open membership. The Cedar Avenue Church of Cleveland adopted it in 1885. In 1903,

Edward Scribner Ames announced open membership for the Hyde Park Church of Christ in Chicago. Other congregations followed suit. By 1919, the Hyde Park Church offered all forms of baptism and even accepted into membership those who had never been baptized at all. Charles Clayton Morrison, Disciples editor of the *Christian Century*, consistently supported open membership in those pages. Meanwhile, by the time of the Pittsburgh Centennial Convention, J. A. Lord, editor at *The Christian Standard*, had changed his mind about the practice and became one of its most articulate opponents.

As Disciples, through their three missionary societies, began to work closely with other Christians and their mission boards, they naturally sought ways to cooperate. Evangelizing the world was a tall order. Disciples knew they could not do it alone. Working with other Christians to do the job naturally fit with their belief in the unity of the church. By the time the UCMS began its work, comity agreements on the mission field were quite routine. Under these agreements, Disciples took responsibility for particular territories, leaving other areas to other Christians.

It didn't take long for Disciples missionaries in China to encounter Chinese Christians who had moved into their comity area from other areas of China where they had been baptized as Congregationalists or Presbyterians. Were they supposed to rebaptize them before welcoming them into the mission? Most Disciples missionaries preferred to accept Christians as Christians regardless of the mode by which they had been baptized.

Union movements in China hoped to promote the open and free interchange of all memberships, ministers, and other workers. Disciples hoped to be included. In 1919, addressing the Kuling Convention in China, missionary G. B. Baird passionately made his point. "I am firmly convinced," Baird preached, "that we should make this move . . . . We dare not continue the position that would force us to continue as an isolated group in China in the midst of a great union movement."

For the next seven years, Disciples fought vigorously over the issue. Officials at home were on the defensive. They were already engaged in a battle with the *Christian Standard* over the formation of the new missionary society. While leaders sympathized with missionary sentiments for union, they decided to forbid open membership on the mission field. Meanwhile, conservative Disciples demanded the recall of any missionaries who favored the practice. They started meeting separately in "congresses" attracting large numbers of Disciples.

Many conservatives began to withdraw financial support from the UCMS. At International Convention gatherings between 1920 and 1925, Disciples passed resolutions to prohibit open membership. In Oklahoma City in 1925, conservatives made their meaning perfectly clear, but felt betrayed again when the interpretation of leaders put a softer edge on the resolution. In Memphis in 1926, a "Commission to the Orient" reported that the UCMS had cleaned up any irregularities in China or the Philippines. For various reasons, many conservatives concluded there had been an intentional cover-up. Disciples were now well on their way to a second major division, though it would take four decades to reach its final form.

By 1927, the "congresses" had turned into the formation of the North American Christian Convention. Though all Disciples were invited to these meetings, they largely attracted those who were inclined not to trust the UCMS. "Cooperative" and "Independent" Disciples emerged. The former continued to support the UCMS and the International Convention, while the latter preferred to work independently of them. Of course, as the North American Christian Convention well demonstrated, the Independents could cooperate with one another in a number of endeavors. More to the point, they opposed the changes taking place within Disciples life, and chose to remain independent from them.

The open membership controversy provided a rallying forum for growing conservative discontent, spurring them to action. Many among them had long been uncomfortable. Open membership merely had provided a third reason for unhappiness. The Disciples tendency toward liberal theology, including critical approaches to the Bible, and new ecumenical commitments provided at least two other reasons. These trends simply did not square well with their understanding of a "restored" church. The way the Independents saw things, the Cooperatives were the ones who had left the building. Many of the same sociological and cultural rifts that played a role in the first split among Disciples also remained a factor in this one.

Disciples generally failed to reflect theologically on their mission during the open membership controversy. UCMS leaders were in sympathy with the union movements in China and the Philippines, but were unable to speak theologically about why. They could have argued that the church belongs to God—that the church is, by its very nature, an inclusive community. When one becomes a Christian, one connects with all other Christians in the body of Christ. Therefore, membership in the community known as the church is not dependent upon any particular form of baptism, but is dependent on one's relationship to Christ. While a few Disciples missionaries made these arguments, their pleas fell on deaf ears. The situation at home was too political; the atmosphere too divisive. Disciples chose to be pragmatic about it. Their pragmatism may only have succeeded in making the division more painful.

Disciples spent considerable efforts over the next forty years trying to repair the breach. In Des Moines in 1934, the International Convention created a commission to "restudy the origin, history, slogans, methods, successes and failures" of the Disciples. The commission on Restudy of the Disciples of Christ, as it was known, had a widely representative membership, including those known as Independents. Reflecting the blind spot operating in most of Disciples life through these years, however, the membership contained no women or representatives of Disciples ethnic communities. The commission met for fourteen years, produced insightful reports about the problems that created challenges to unity within Disciples. Yet in the end, it could not resolve the crisis between the Cooperatives and the Independents. Still, the commission provided a model of cooperation between the two groups that has lived on through cooperative involvement by both groups in such organizations as the Pension Fund (1928), the World Convention of Churches of Christ (1930), and the Disciples of Christ Historical Society (1941).

In the face of these internal challenges, and in spite of the additional challenge known as the Great Depression, the UCMS accomplished significant work on the mission field. Between 1920 and 1946, membership grew from 23,711 to 81,653. From roughly 3 self-supporting congregations located in foreign mission stations in 1923, the Disciples could count 635 by 1946. Disciples educated an average of more than 15,000 students a year on the mission field during this period. Disciples did, however, get much greater productivity out of a much smaller missionary staff, which had dropped from a high of 339 workers in 1925 to about 202 by 1946.

145

THE THEOLOGY OF MISSION

The period after World War II had been a vibrant period for American theology. By mid-century, Disciples also began to struggle in earnest with theological themes circulating in American Protestantism. Increasingly Disciples biblical theologians, historians, and ministers engaged the work produced by neo-orthodox and existentialist theologians working in America and in places like Germany and England. A new concern for theological reflection showed up

W. Barnett Blakemore

most notably in the work of the Panel of Scholars (1957-1961). The panel met for four years to present papers on nearly every aspect of Disciples life and to place them in a context that took theological reflection seriously. In 1963, W. Barnett Blakemore served as general editor for the publication of these papers in a three-volume series under the title *The Renewal of the Church*. The articles focused on three themes:the place of theology in Disciples life, the nature of the church, and the role of Christ.

James Duke and Joseph Driskill concluded that these books made contributions in at least two areas. First, they offered the observation that Disciples had a tradition, and "that tradition is Jesus Christ." This freed the scholars to connect with the whole history of Christian theology as it sought to understand the work of Christ. Yet, only a few of the essays demonstrate an ability to do so. More of the essays still tended to rely on the work of the Campbells and other early founders. As Sheila Hope Gillams noted in her doctoral dissertation, this meant that most of them remained indifferent to matters of race. For example, nowhere in these pages will one find notice of the burgeoning civil rights movement.

Second, the Panel of Scholars modeled a new freedom to develop contemporary and public theological understandings that challenged the tradition in order to understand what it meant to affirm Christ during the 1950s. For example, theologian Ralph Wilburn critically

146

engaged the theological trends swirling in Protestantism at the time. His work stressed the relativities of everything human, "the church itself, . . . its scriptures and traditions, its structures of polity, rites, programs, and all the rest."

Though Disciples continued to struggle with issues related to systemic racism, their theological renaissance during the 1950s created a context that enabled a reconsideration of the meaning of both mission and polity among the Disciples. Disciples had long ignored attending to a theological understanding of world mission. Finally, during the 1950s, they began to tend to it. The major impetus to theological reflection grew from the 1952 World Meeting of the International Missionary Council at Willengen, Germany.

At this meeting, younger churches, located in developing countries where people struggled to cast off the yoke of Western colonialism, asked missionary organizations to forgo their attitude of paternalism in order to embody a new spirit of partnership. Younger churches sought greater freedom from the control of missionary organizations, especially since most people in the revolutionary world understood mission work as one more example of colonial power. In response to this call, Virgil Sly led the foreign division of the United Christian Missionary Society (UCMS) in a reconsideration of its theology of missions. He was aided in this work by study papers prepared by a new Commission on the Theology of Mission (1958-1962), co-sponsored by both the UCMS and the Council on Christian Unity. In 1956, Sly changed the name of the "Division of Foreign Missions" to the "Division of World Mission." By 1959, he had also changed the title of "The Strategy for World Missions," a document first developed in 1955, to "The Strategy for World Mission." These changes, in Sly's words, resulted from the recognition that "the mission . . . is God's mission." With this shift, Disciples stopped thinking of their work as creating "missions" in foreign locations and sought instead to serve as witnesses to the work of God's mission which began in every location in the world long before any Christian presence had ever appeared.

THE THEOLOGY OF CHURCH

The theological renaissance during the 1950s also led Disciples to a reconsideration of their church organization. Just as the Panel of

147

Scholars finished its work, Disciples established a Commission on Brotherhood Restructure. The chaos of Disciples organized life, with its many competing national agencies and state societies, obviously contributed to the desire for a more effective church structure. However, it is also true that conclusions reached by the Panel of Scholars, particularly the recognition that the Disciples emphasis on congregational autonomy reflected life on the American frontier more than it did any particular biblical model of church life, helped provide rationale for considering this kind of move. The commission committed itself to think theologically about its task.

The commission began with an examination of the biblical metaphors for the church. This approach brought to mind the church's dependence upon Christ (Body of Christ), the initiative of God in creating and sustaining the work of the church (Household of God), and the responsibility of the church as witness to God's redeeming work in the world (Servant of God). These metaphors reminded the commission that the church exists in the covenant of God's love made clear in Christ, and that Christians are responsible both to one another and to the mission of God's reconciliation in history.

Ronald Osborn (1917–1998) led the commission to understand the proper place for theology in considering a matter like church structure. He set forth three theses: (1) No doctrine of the church can dictate the complete details of any church structure; theological reflection has limits; (2) every doctrine of the church contains implications for church structure, and every church structure contains theological implications; and (3) because theology has limits, pragmatic questions must also be considered; "common sense and practical experience" should operate where theology has nothing particular to add. For example, the question of the number of regions might be decided on pragmatic grounds alone, the question of whether delegates within these regions ought to include women and men, minister

Ronald Osborn

148

and lay, and racial-ethnic representation is best decided on theological grounds.

The work of the Commission on Restructure concluded on September 26, 1968, when Disciples voted in Kansas City to accept the new *Provisional Design* outlining a new structure. Adoption of the *Design* formally changed the notion of "church" operating in Disciples life. With this restructure, Disciples shifted from a notion of gathered congregations (churches) to an understanding of the gathered church, composed of congregations living in covenant with one another. The formal name of Disciples shifted from Christian Churches (Disciples of Christ) to the Christian Church (Disciples of Christ). When this covenant is understood in the context of the universal body of Christ (the church), the parenthetical "Disciples of Christ" recognizes that Disciples do not constitute the whole church, but only one partial and fragmentary expression of it.

This new polity finally permanently divided the Disciples from the Independents. Perhaps with some justification, many among Independents argued the move reflected more a Disciples desire for status among the mainline denominations than it did a new theological understanding of the church. Over the six-year period from 1967-1972, some thirty-five-hundred congregations composed of approximately 750,000 members, withdrew from the Disciples year book. They formed a new church body known as the Christian Churches and Churches of Christ. Their departure affected Disciples numbers, but not Disciples giving. Most of them had stopped supporting Disciples common work decades earlier. During the five years of their formal departure, Disciples giving to outreach increased by 1.3 million dollars.

The diversity of Disciples theological perspectives and their church life grew considerably after the mid-1960s, alongside an awakening cultural awareness of the complexity of religious pluralism within American life itself.

FOR FURTHER READING

Cummins, D. Duane. *The Disciples: A Struggle for Reformation*. St. Louis: Chalice Press, 2009. See pages 155-223.

Duke, James O. and Joseph D. Driskill. "Disciples Theologizing amid Currents of Mainstream Protestant Thought, 1940-1980: Sketchbook Observations." In D. Newell Williams. *A Case Study of Mainstream Protestantism: The Disciples Relation to American Culture, 1880-1989*. Grand Rapids: Eerdmans, 1991. See pages 139-164.

Gillams, Sheila Hope. "Principle and Practice: The Quandary of African American Restorationists in the History and Theology of the Church of Christ, Disciples of Christ, 1850-1950." Ph.D. diss., Union Theological Seminary, New York City, 2002.

Smith, Joseph. "A Strategy of World Mission: The Theory and Practice of Mission as Seen in the Present World Mission Enterprise of the Disciples of Christ." Th.D. diss., Union Theological Seminary, 1961.

Toulouse, Mark G. *Joined in Discipleship: The Shaping of Contemporary Disciples Identity*. St. Louis: Chalice Press, 1997. See pages 189-244.

Toulouse, Mark G. "Practical Concern and Theological Neglect: The UCMS and the Open Membership Controversy." In D. Newell Williams, *A Case Study of Mainstream Protestantism: The Disciples Relation to American Culture, 1880-1989*. Grand Rapids: Eerdmans, 1991. See pages 194-235.

QUESTIONS FOR DISCUSSION

1. Why did concerns about the structure of the church emerge during this period? What did Disciples do to meet those concerns, first early in the century and then shortly after mid-century?

2. What kinds of challenges did women in leadership face as the twentieth century opened?

3. How did the open membership controversy emerge, and how did it affect Disciples life during these years?

4. In what ways did Disciples come to understand the concept of mission differently during the twentieth century?

5. How would you describe the meaning of the name "The Christian Church (Disciples of Christ)"—for example, what is the role played by the parenthesis in the name?

Chapter

THE CHALLENGES POSED BY
DECLINE AND IDENTITY

In 1948, Disciples listed over 1.7 million members. Their growth throughout the nineteenth century and early twentieth century had been phenomenal. Through additions, baptismal or otherwise, Disciples averaged adding in excess of 100,000 new members each year. They had over 8,000 ministers and more than 7,800 congregations. As of May 2009, Disciples reported about 681,480 members. Of these, some 435,070 are designated as "participating members." About 221,600 Disciples across North America attended worship on a fairly regular basis in 2010. The numbers of members associated with Disciples have declined considerably over the past sixty years.

Today's Disciples can still count about 7,010 ministers, but the number of congregations regularly reporting to Disciples number around 2,571. It is important to remember that, between 1967 and 1972, around 750,000 "Independent" Disciples, and in the neighborhood of 3,500 congregations, formally left the movement and aligned with the newly formed Christian Churches and Churches of Christ. But even after this exodus, the 1975 Disciples Year Book reported 1,317,044 members through May 1974. The decline in Disciples numbers since the mid-1970s has been dramatic, an average of about 18,700 members per year. To put these numbers in perspective, this is equivalent to shutting down a 360-member Disciples congregation every Sunday for thirty-four consecutive years. Disciples have lost about 48.3% of their membership since 1974. By comparison, the United Church of Christ has lost roughly

43% of its membership during the same period. Most of the "mainline" Protestant denominations across North America can tell the same story during these years, so Disciples are not at all unique in this respect.

THE NATURE OF TRENDS AND THE CAUSES OF DECLINE

Kenneth Teegarden (1921-2002), General Minister and President for Disciples from 1973 to 1985, enjoyed saying that the trends indicated the last living Disciples church member ought to be able to inherit all church assets sometime in 2042. However, as Teegarden knew well, trends are not realities. For example, when Elvis Presley died in 1977, there were 170 Elvis Presley impersonators. Today, there are more than 50,000. If the trend continues, by the year 2025, one out of every three people in North America will be an Elvis Presley impersonator. Obviously, when trends are used to predict the future with an assumed precision, the result can be absurd. Yet, trends serve a useful purpose. Examining trends can help a church decide what needs nurturing and what needs to be nipped in the bud.

Kenneth Teegarden

In the 1970s a considerable shift in southward population and industry occurred in the United States. The Sunbelt became the most powerful section of the country, driving most every aspect of its life, including the office of the presidency. Beginning with Lyndon Baines Johnson in 1963, five of the nine most recent presidents were born in the South or Southwest. The other four were born in California, Nebraska, Illinois, and Hawaii. Not a single one of the last nine presidents of the United States, since 1963, hail from the eastern seaboard.

As a side note, two of these presidents, Johnson and Reagan, were both Disciples of Christ. Their clear political differences and approaches demonstrate the wide range of social and political beliefs found among Disciples in the later twentieth century. Their religious connection to Disciples life illustrates the extent to which the denomination itself has entered into mainstream American public and political life. The fact that President Barack Obama chose Sharon Watkins, current President and General Minister for Disciples, to deliver the sermon for the National Prayer Service that capped his inaugural festivities also illustrates this point. While Disciples have enjoyed their "mainstream" status, they have continued to experience rapid decline in membership.

Since the mid-1970s, large numbers of people have moved to Florida, Georgia, North Carolina, Texas, Colorado, Arizona, and California. Most of the old mainline Protestant denominations (the Presbyterian Church in the USA, the United Methodist Church, the American Baptists, the Episcopal Church, the Evangelical Lutheran Church of America, the United Church of Christ, and the Disciples) are primarily located in the states that lost population. On the other hand, evangelical and non-denominational Protestantism, both powerhouses in Southern religion, benefitted from this shift in people and finances. As a result of these geographical shifts, the highest numbers of members and congregations are now located in Texas and part of New Mexico, in the Southern region of the country. The next highest populous regions for Disciples are in Indiana, northern Missouri, southern Illinois, Ohio, and Kentucky. The greatest concentration of Disciples in relation to the population of an area is today found in the Kansas City region.

A shift in population and business, of course, does not tell the whole story. The fastest growing category in American religion is "unaffiliated," growing from roughly 2% of the population in 1967 to 16.1% in 2007. Other studies have shown that many of these "unaffiliated" continue to read scriptures associated with some religious tradition or another, and about one-third claim to pray regularly. Many today find spiritual experiences outside of any organized church or faith community. Others have found substitute faiths in such locations as yoga classes, martial arts exercises, or in such organizations as Common Cause, the Sierra Club, or Greenpeace. If one were entirely honest about the early 1970s, one would recognize that a good number of the members of Protestant churches were there because it was the "cultural thing" to do. That era has certainly passed.

Finally, the cultural shifts begun in the 1960s have also contributed to these shifts in religious alignments. The importance of the civil rights struggle, the rising of feminist consciousness, and social developments like birth control and changing understandings of human sexuality have all affected religious alignments. Further, since the 1965 changes in immigration policy in the United States, the importance and presence of religious pluralism has exploded. American culture has become significantly more pluralistic.

By the end of the 1960s, the fragmentation of Protestantism and the increased diversity of America's religions led many to believe that public life in America must be free of Protestant or even Christian associations. Today, Los Angeles contains a more diverse assortment of Buddhist temples and membership than any other city in the world. Traditional Protestant values no longer benefit from close connections with American culture. Disciples, like other Protestant groups, began directing more of their attention to the importance of interfaith discussion and relationships. Clark Williamson, in his work as a Disciples theologian, has contributed to the development of a Post-*Shoah* (or Post-Holocaust) theology in order to challenge centuries of anti-Semitism within Christian theology. The Council on Christian Unity among Disciples has also published "Disciples of Christ and Interfaith Engagement," in order to encourage Disciples "wholeheartedly to engage in interfaith relations and work."

Other Contemporary Challenges

Disciples, like everyone else in church life, have been affected by the downturn in the economy. In the past decade, the national work of Disciples, represented in the general units of the church's life, has experienced a considerable downsizing. When the Disciples restructured in 1968, creating a more organized and connected church, they did not provide for the kind of accountability and financial support needed to sustain the work of the new church. Yet, neither could they have foreseen the kinds of cultural shifts that led to both declining membership and finances. Many Christians now prefer to keep their dollars closer to home; they like to see close-up the kinds of ministries their dollars finance.

More bad news hit Disciples in 2002 when the Christian Board of Publication (CBP) stopped publishing *The Disciple*, the monthly magazine for Disciples of Christ. Affected by the same financial constraints, the CBP had to make measured cuts where it could. A group of Disciples leaders, led by James Suggs and Robert Friedly, created a new magazine called *DisciplesWorld* to fill the gap. The latter magazine carried on valiantly for nearly eight years until February 2010. Partly the victim of the same financial forces affecting all church life generally, *DisciplesWorld* also faced the same factors creating rapid decline of print journalism everywhere. In the digital age, most newspapers and magazines have difficulty keeping up.

The biggest shock for Disciples arrived in 2004 when the National Benevolent Association (NBA) filed for bankruptcy. At one time the pride and joy of Disciples home mission work, managing more than ninety-five facilities located in twenty-two states, the NBA became overextended when it expanded into upscale senior care facilities. The growing instability of its investments due to market fluctuations contributed to a difficult economic situation from which it could not recover. Following a period of reorganization, the NBA, today known as Disciples Benevolent Services, is now a much smaller organization, overseeing a few facilities and coordinating work with other organizations in a few cities across the country.

Mission funding in the United States for Disciples work fell by more than 10% between 1993 and 2003 alone, from just over 33 million to just under 30 million. In response to developments like these, Disciples have had to make adjustments. Over the past two decades, general and regional offices of the church's life have been engaged in a process of cutting both personnel and programs. Yet, through it all, Disciples have worked to remain focused on mission and ministry.

The Response of Disciples to Decline

Disciples divide their church's work into three areas working within a voluntary and covenantal arrangement: the local, the regional, and the general. Congregations control their own affairs and support various ministries of their own choosing. Most contribute something financially to support the regional and general work. Disciples have thirty-three regions across the United States and

Canada. Regional and general offices support congregations and provide for cooperation in wider ministries.

General church work among Disciples is managed by a General Assembly that meets every other year. A General Board does planning for the church in between assemblies. Various general units specialize in ministries related to such things as higher education, home missions, global ministries, and benevolence work. Other offices administer the church's pension fund, the Disciples Mission Fund, and the permanent funds supporting the general and regional ministries. Disciples provide around twenty-five million dollars annually, on top of operating costs, for local, regional, and general church outreach ministries.

Due to their commitment to an educated faith, Disciples sponsor fourteen colleges and universities, containing some 27,000 students, and four theological seminaries. Each of these schools is diverse, with the vast numbers of students coming from religious affiliations other than Disciples. Three other colleges maintain an historic relationship with the Disciples of Christ even though they no longer receive denominational funding (Drake University, Northwest Christian University, and Tougaloo College). Disciples also maintain support for three "foundation" houses located at the University of Chicago, Vanderbilt University, and in Claremont, California. These houses support Disciples students engaged in graduate work in non-Disciples settings.

The 2020 Vision

Under the leadership of former General Minister and President, Richard Hamm, Disciples created something they call the "2020 Vision" articulating goals they want to accomplish by the year 2020. The core values of this vision identify three marks of the faithful church: true community, a deep Christian spirituality, and a passion for justice. Under Hamm's leadership, Disciples set four priorities: to become a pro-reconciling and anti-racist church; to establish 1,000 new congregations by the year 2020; to transform 1,000 existing congregations by 2020; and to provide the kind of leadership development necessary to sustain these new and renewed congregations. These four initiatives have paid dividends. The number of Disciples congregations increased for three years in a row, from 2003 to 2005. As of 2007, Disciples were halfway on their way to 1,000 new congregations, three years ahead of the 2020 schedule.

Disciples are also beginning to stem their decline in numbers. The two-year period from May 2002 to May 2004 showed a drop in members of 48,365; the two-year period from May 2004 to May 2006 dropped 42,579 members; but the two year period from May 2006 to May 2008 only dropped 16,541. This last two year period is only about 34.2% of the drop suffered from 2002 to 2004.

THE NATURE OF DISCIPLES IDENTITY

Disciples, like other mainline groups, are at work trying to develop meaningful strategies to help both existing and new congregations understand the meaning of Christian identity. It seems like an obvious question: What are congregations among Disciples doing to help members understand what it means to be Christian? What does your congregation do to make you think about the profound differences between Christian identity and your identity as a good-hearted American citizen, or a philanthropically-minded person who attends church with people who think just like you do, or who is middle-class like you, or high-class like you, or poor like you, or who looks just like you? What is your congregation doing to help you think about how Christian identity transforms and challenges us to be different than what we would be if we weren't Christian? Or, does the brand of Christian identity we practice simply reaffirm and reinforce our personal biases, ideas, and practices of life and work?

Under the leadership of Sharon Watkins, General Minister and President for Disciples since 2005, Disciples have begun to work out a common understanding of the meaning of their Christian identity. In her first year, Watkins created a "21st Century Vision Team" and asked members to examine the church's identity, mission, and structure. The

Sharon Watkins

159

team produced a two-sentence statement along with twelve principles defining more fully the nature of identity among Disciples. From July 2007 to March 2008, more than 1,450 Disciples responded to the statement by completing an online survey. The statement on identity met with wide approval from those who responded. In its final form, the statement reads as follows:

Statement of Identity

We are Disciples of Christ, a movement for wholeness in a fragmented world. As part of the one body of Christ, we welcome all to the Lord's Table as God has welcomed us.

Principles of Identity

1. We confess that Jesus is the Christ, the Son of the Living God, and proclaim him Lord and Savior of the world, requiring nothing more—and nothing less—as a basis of our life together.
2. We hold the centrality of scripture, recognizing that each person has the freedom—and the responsibility—to study God's Word within the community of the church.
3. We practice the baptism of believers, which emphasizes that God's grace demands a response of faith and discipleship, while also recognizing the baptism performed in other churches.
4. We gather for the Lord's Supper, as often as possible, experiencing at this table the gracious, forgiving presence of Jesus Christ.
5. We structure our community around the biblical idea of covenant, emphasizing not obedience to human authority but accountability to one another because of our shared obedience to Christ.
6. We participate in God's mission for the world, working with partners to heal the brokenness of creation and bring justice and peace to the whole human family.
7. We hear a special calling to make visible the unity of all Christians, proclaiming that in our diversity we belong to one another because we commonly belong to Christ.

8. We witness to the Gospel of God's saving love for the world in Jesus Christ, while continuing to struggle with how God's love may be known to others in different ways.
9. We affirm the priesthood of all believers, rejoicing in the gifts of the Holy Spirit—which include the gift of leadership— that God has given for the common good.
10. We celebrate the diversity of our common life, affirming our different histories, styles of worship, and forms of service.
11. We give thanks that each congregation, where Christ is present through faith, is truly the church, affirming as well that God's church and God's mission stretch from our doorsteps to the ends of the earth.
12. We anticipate God's coming reign, seeking to serve the God—Creator, Redeemer, and Sustainer—whose loving dominion has no end.

Though the Disciples have long been active in mission, many of the successful mission activities of congregations and the denomination were often disconnected from an explicit theological understanding of Christian identity. When mission responds to the poor, the hungry, the sick, and the homeless, how does the church respond in ways that are different from the responses of many secular social agencies? How does the church engage in outreach that effectively communicates an understanding of what it means to be a child of God? Do Disciples congregations have a clear sense of the entirety of the church's responsibility of witness in the name of Christ to the whole inhabited earth? The mission of the church is only possible where Christian identity is affirmed and expressed. And it can only be accomplished through a recognition that the mission is God's, not our own. How do we talk about God's mission, and our frail efforts to support it, if we don't have a clear sense, theologically, of who God is and who we are?

The Protestant mainline has learned much from the development of anti-establishment theologies including feminist, black, and other liberation theologies. These theological developments have taught some congregations to stress inclusivity and work toward justice. They have helped to transform inherited concepts of mission and to provide a much more globally aware church life. In some ways, Disciples are now situated on the fringes of American religious life.

There is nothing inherently negative about that location. The power of culture over the church's life is minimized when the church no longer stands at the center of culture. But it does not necessarily follow that the power of the church's voice is minimized when it speaks from the fringes rather than the center. Freed of its cultural attachments, the church might be better able to concentrate on a renewal of what is most important to its future: the effort to gain a clearer sense of both Christian identity and Christian mission.

As members of a Christian tradition that stands in the midst of a culture that values pluralism (sometimes having the effect of moving Christian concerns from the center to the edges of the culture), can Disciples of Christ speak powerfully about their identity to the communities around them? Disciples hope their church life will reflect their beliefs that the church is one, that God cares for and about the development of human history, that grace surprises human beings in unexpected ways and brings redemption at precisely the points they are tempted simply to give up. When the church lives on the fringes of American culture, it is offered the grand opportunity to speak in public about the way the principles of Christian faith, rather than principles derived from the culture, define the church's relationship to the public life Christians share with others in the United States. But to do this, Christians must have an understanding of their own Christian identity. They must nurture that identity in order to bring clarity to what it means to be Christian and to the public expressions that provide witness to it. In recent years, Disciples have worked to develop more conscientious efforts to understand their Christian identity, to take it seriously, and to represent it faithfully in all that they do.

FOR FURTHER READING:

Council on Christian Unity. "Disciples of Christ and Interreligious Engagement." This report can be found on the following Web site: http://www.disciples.org/ccu/PDF/Disciples%20of%20Christ%20 and%20Interreligious%20Engagement.pdf

Cummins, D. Duane. *The Disciples: A Struggle for Reformation*. St. Louis: Chalice Press, 2009. See pages 248-272.

Hamm, Richard L. *2020 Vision for the Christian Church (Disciples of Christ)*. St. Louis: Chalice Press, 2001.

Kinnamon, Michael and Jan G. Linn. *Disciples: Reclaiming Our Identity, Reforming Our Practice*. St. Louis: Chalice Press, 2009.

Toulouse, Mark G. *Joined In Discipleship: The Shaping of Contemporary Disciples Identity*. St. Louis: Chalice Press, 1997. See pages 245-278.

Williamson, Clark. *A Guest in the House of Israel: Post Holocaust Church Theology*. Louisville: Westminster John Knox Press, 1993.

QUESTIONS FOR DISCUSSION

1. How would you describe the challenges faced by Disciples of Christ in the last half century?

2. Why do you think Disciples of Christ and other so-called mainline churches have declined in memberships so dramatically since the late 1960s?

3. What steps have Disciples of Christ taken to respond to these challenges?

4. What is your response to the new "Statement of Identity" for Disciples? What do you think is missing? Is there anything you would say differently? Can you describe in a paragraph what you believe to be the essence of Christian identity for Disciples?

5. How might a renewed emphasis on Christian identity help Disciples to engage interfaith discussions responsibly?

Chapter 14

DIVERSITY IN THE MIDST OF UNITY

As this book has demonstrated, Disciples have struggled with the meaning of diversity throughout their life as a church. From a time when white males controlled every aspect of the life of the church and its ministry, Disciples now reflect, increasingly with each passing year, a different kind of reality. Women were, of course, the first group to teach the white males a thing or two about leadership. Their highly successful endeavors in mission organization and support in the late nineteenth century set the standard for the next generation of leadership. Yet it has still taken a long time for Disciples to take full advantage of the gifts of women in the ministry of the church. Though large numbers of women served in ministry on the mission field, only a few broke through to serve churches as ministers at home. In 1973, only eight women were listed as pastors of more than 2,650 recognized congregations. By 2007, 887 women served as either fulltime pastors or associate ministers, or as student pastors or student associates, more than 29% of the total number of those who served in these positions.

In addition to their roles as pastors and church leaders, Disciples women in more recent decades have contributed significantly as academic leaders and theologians. For several decades, Rita Nakashima Brock has provided significant leadership for the development of North American feminist theology. As a leading theologian who also possesses Asian and Hispanic roots, Brock has emphasized the need to reclaim the empowering characteristics of Christian theology. "The heart of Christianity," she wrote in 1988, "must be reinterpreted in nonoppressive ways if Christianity's

165

greatest promise is not to remain its greatest problem, not just for women, but for all who seek to liberate the present." Through their daily work, Disciples scholars like Brock (an independent scholar), Serene Jones (Union Theological Seminary), Kris Culp (University of Chicago), Bonnie Miller-McLemore (Vanderbilt Divinity School), Claudia Camp (Texas Christian University), Nadia Lahusky (Texas Christian University), and others have educated a new generation of Disciples undergraduates and ministers in theology, pastoral care, Bible, and church history.

Since the 1960s, ethnic diversity has become far more prominent in Disciples life as well. Not all contemporary Disciples congregations have declined in membership. Many ethnic congregations have experienced considerable growth. In fact, when one considers statistical categories in general, those dealing with ethnic diversity among Disciples have defied all the downward trends plaguing the main life of the church. Haitian Disciples in New York, Korean Disciples in California, and Hispanic Disciples in the southern portions of the country have all seen strong growth. Some of the largest congregations among contemporary Disciples are predominantly African American. Though Hispanic and Asian Disciples are considerably fewer in number than African American Disciples, their growth in the last few decades has also been impressive.

AFRICAN AMERICAN DISCIPLES

Though connected to the Disciples from the beginning of the movement's history, African American Disciples experienced difficulty in achieving a prominent voice within denominational life.

In the 1940s, black leaders began to knock on the door of Disciples educational institutions seeking further education. Emmett J. Dickson and R. H. Peoples both applied to the Disciples House at the University of Chicago for fellowships. Both were turned down. After a time of controversy covered well by *The Christian Plea*, a journal attending to life among black Disciples, William K. Fox, a graduate of Tennessee State College, applied for entrance to the University of Chicago Divinity School. The university accepted him and granted him a divinity school scholarship, but the Disciples house located there did not grant a fellowship providing for housing and a stipend. More controversy ensued.

166

Near the end of his first year, Edward Scribner Ames called Fox and informed him he would receive a fellowship from Disciples House for the remainder of his studies.

By 1956, there were 556 black Disciple congregations with over 51,000 members. An additional 791 black Disciples were members in other congregations. In 1956, black disciples constituted about 3.18% of Disciples membership. Until 1960, African American Disciples had separate agencies and programs in most areas of church life. By 1969,

William K. Fox

Disciples merged the National Christian Missionary Convention and the newly established Christian Church (Disciples of Christ). In 1970, black Disciples formed the National Convocation of the Christian Church that has, since that time, met every other year to discuss their special concerns. Black Disciples have provided significant leadership in every area of Disciples life in the contemporary period. Names like John Compton (the first African-American board member of the UCMS), Raymond E. Brown (served as Senior Vice-President of Church Extension, and in many other capacities in the general church throughout a long career), Emmett J. Dickson (faculty member at Jarvis College and later served as National Director of Church Relations in the UCMS), Kenneth Henry (longtime faculty member at Interdenominational Theological Center in Atlanta) and many others, are well known in Disciples church circles.

In 2008, there were approximately 440 African American Disciples congregations containing approximately 40,000 participating members, about 9.2% of Disciples in that category. Three African American congregations, led by ministers Bishop T. Garrott Benjamin, Dr. Cynthia Hale, and Dr. Frank Thomas, are among the largest congregations among Disciples, with memberships of more than 2,000 each (Light of the World in Indianapolis, Indiana; Ray of Hope in Decatur, Georgia; and Mississippi Boulevard in Memphis, Tennessee).

HISPANIC DISCIPLES

Daisy Machado has demonstrated well how Disciples in the early twentieth century largely neglected to provide a meaningful ministry to serve the growing numbers of Hispanics in the southwest. As had been true of Native Americans and African Americans, as Disciples began to wake up to Hispanic needs and sought to provide some small measure of benevolent services, they often expressed needs by referring to the "Mexican problem." Until the latter part of the twentieth century, Disciples did not make many efforts to provide Spanish-speaking ministers in Texas or in Florida. Hispanics created Disciples congregations on their own, the first in San Antonio in 1899. By 1916, seven Disciples Hispanic congregations created a convention, but financial needs were so great, they could not accomplish much. In the mid-1950s, there were only ten Disciples Hispanic congregations with about 636 members. A larger number of Latina/Latino Disciples were spread throughout other congregations. Around 1950, large numbers of Puerto Ricans began settling in the United States, most of them in New York City. Many of these new immigrants had been members of the Disciples in Puerto Rico before arriving in the United States. Since the mid-1950s, Disciples in Puerto Rico had provided their own leadership, independent of Disciples in the United States.

Puerto Rican Disciples established their own congregations when they arrived in New York. In 1939, La Hermosa Christian Church in New York City became the first of these congregations. Originally, the congregation did not have a formal association with Disciples. When the church hired Pablo Cotto, a Disciples minister from Puerto Rico, the congregation connected to Disciples and became the "mother church" for most Hispanic Disciples in the northeastern part of the country. Over the years, La Hermosa has helped to establish a number of other Disciples congregations, and assisted other independent Latina/Latino congregations in connecting to Disciples. By the end of the 1960s, more than one-third of all Disciples congregations in New York City were Spanish-speaking. Many of today's key leaders for Latina/Latino Disciples are originally from Puerto Rico.

In 1981, growing out of an office previously located in the Division of Homeland Ministries of the UCMS, Hispanic Disciples formed a National Hispanic and Bilingual Fellowship. Strong leadership has been provided for this work during the last fifty years by people like Domingo Rodriguez (b. 1918), Lucas Torres (b. 1933), David Vargas (b. 1944) and Pablo A. Jimenez (b. 1960). In 2003, Hispanic Disciples could boast of approximately 123 congregations, about fifty of which had been developed within the last two years. In 2009, there were about 7,500 participating Hispanic Disciples in about 155 congregations. Central Florida saw the largest growth. In 1975, there were no Hispanic Disciples congregations in Florida; by 2003, there were six congregations in central Florida alone attracting over 1,500 people every Sunday. A full one-third of all Disciples in Florida in 2003 were Hispanics.

ASIAN AMERICAN DISCIPLES

Disciples reflected the same cultural prejudices toward Asians. Yet, North American churches, Disciples among them, were among the few cultural institutions that connected at all with the needs of Asian immigrant communities. Sometime between 1889 and 1891, the Christian Woman's Board of Missions (CWBM) connected with the First Christian Church of Portland to open a Chinese Christian Mission. The work constituted the first connection between Disciples and the Asian community. The community grew rapidly and came under the leadership of a Chinese pastor, educated at Drake, named Jeu Hawk. The CWBM founded a similar mission in 1907 in San Francisco. Work with Japanese immigrants began a year later in Los Angeles. By 1933, Disciples began mission work among Filipinos in Los Angeles who developed a congregation that weathered the difficulties of the twentieth century and continues to exist. Before the war, a number of other Japanese congregations emerged. All these were closed in connection to events surrounding World War II.

Jeu Hawk

169

With the change of immigration legislation in 1965, Asians were allowed to arrive in the United States on the same basis as Europeans and others. With the help of leaders like Harold Johnson (b. 1921) and David Kagiwada (1929-1985), Asian Disciples began organizing in the late 1970s when they developed the Fellowship of Asian American Disciples. Johnson served as the Director of Evangelism with the Division of Homeland Ministries; and Kagiwada, a second generation Japanese American, had been in an internment camp during the war. NAPAD and Disciples have also benefitted from the effective ministries of people like Soongook Choi (1933-2002) and Jaikwan Ahn (b. 1930). Since 1992, Geunhee Yu, who holds a PhD from Vanderbilt Divinity School, has provided leadership for Asian Disciples. In 1996, the organization became known as the North American Pacific Asian Disciples (NAPAD) and assumed a prominent place in the life of the denomination.

When Yu assumed leadership in 1992, there were eight congregations identified with the Fellowship of Asian American Disciples. By 2003, there were approximately seventy-five NAPAD congregations, fifty-eight of them Korean (about 3,500 members). The remaining congregations consist mostly of Filipino, Chinese, Vietnamese, Japanese, Indonesian, Laotian, and Samoan churches (approximately another 1,000 members). By 2008, there were eighty-five NAPAD congregations with approximately 5,000 members. In addition, there are a number of Asian and Pacific Islanders who are members of Disciples congregations not directly affiliated with NAPAD.

DIVERSITY IN SEXUAL ORIENTATION

Yet another form of diversity has emerged among Disciples since the 1960s. Most mainline denominational groups have struggled with the question of sexual orientation since the gay liberation movement first emerged in the 1960s. Illinois became the first state to decriminalize homosexual acts between consenting adults in 1963. This began a cultural move to recognize that civil rights should include the rights of persons of differing sexual orientations. In 1973, the American Psychiatric Association dropped homosexuality from its list of mental disorders. Such cultural changes caused churches to begin to consider the question of sexual orientation more seriously.

Some North American churches began to provide targeted ministries for the homosexual community. Glide Memorial Church, a Methodist congregation in San Francisco, was among the most successful of these early ministries. Other church leaders began to take the step of defending the civil rights of gays and lesbians without condoning their lifestyles. Still others took more progressive steps. In November 1967, a gathering of ninety Episcopal priests met at the Cathedral of St. John the Divine in New York to issue a statement urging the church to define same-sex acts between consenting adults as "morally neutral" and to acknowledge the possibility that these acts might actually be good as they represented love between two persons.

The mainline church has argued over the role of gays and lesbians in the church since the 1960s. The United Church of Christ became the first denomination to ordain an openly gay person when the church ordained William Reagan Johnson on June 27, 1972. By the late 1970s, most of the mainline churches were engaged in major studies of the subject. In 1977, meeting in General Assembly in Kansas City, Disciples passed a resolution urging civil rights for all persons, regardless of sexual orientation. The same General Assembly, after considerable debate and controversy on the floor, also passed a study document on the topic recommended to the churches for reading and reflection. Two other resolutions failed to pass at the assembly, one condemning homosexuality as a lifestyle and the other denying ordination to any candidate who either practices or expresses a preference for homosexual behavior. In 1979, the General Assembly meeting in St. Louis revisited the issue to note that, while Disciples as a whole are not yet convinced that ordination of gays and lesbians "is in accord with God's will for the Church," the matter of determining fitness and the responsibility for oversight of ministry rested with the regions and not with the general church.

In the intervening years, the majority of the thirty-three Disciples regions have passed prohibitions related to ordaining practicing homosexuals while a few regions have stated policies indicating that no particular human condition is an absolute barrier to ordination. The Northern California-Nevada region provided

171

leadership when, in 1993, it passed a resolution encouraging congregations to "Welcome all persons, regardless of sexual orientation, into church membership with all of its privileges and responsibilities, including full opportunities for positions of leadership and ministry, subject to the biblical qualifications for all peoples." In more recent years, ordination committees in a few Disciples regions have ordained openly gay women and men to successful ministries in the church.

Disciples have possessed a long history of struggling with their witness on behalf of social justice. In more recent years, since about the 1970s, resolutions in the General Assembly have sought to address abortion, human rights, genocide, civil liberties, and more recently, resolutions questioning, for example, the appropriateness of the war in Iraq and Israeli settlements on the west bank. Disciples have long struggled with applying their faith to the issues affecting human beings in every aspect of community life. These resolutions are usually surrounded by controversial discussion and dialogue, but quite often have resulted in a significant witness to the gospel during days when the culture has stood in the midst of this or that social crisis. Disciples, as well, through the struggle with controversy, have learned to take their identity as Christians more seriously in thinking about contemporary moral issues.

MODERN DISCIPLES AND UNITY

In addition to learning the importance of taking seriously the diversity within their own midst, Disciples have continued to work on affirming the diversity of Christian witness across the world. In recent decades, Disciples have continued to participate fully in a large variety of ecumenical organizations. The General Assembly of Disciples affirmed documents, like *Baptism, Eucharist, Ministry* (1982, World Council of Churches) working toward theological consensus between denominations. Disciples have also produced documents of their own, adjusting their theological and ecumenical understanding of such topics as authority, baptism, ministry, and the Lord's Supper. In their study of baptism in 1987, Disciples meeting in General Assembly officially recognized infant baptism as a legitimate form of baptism and endorsed the ecumenical understanding that those baptized as infants should not be re-baptized.

172

One of the most noteworthy ecumenical involvements in recent years has been their relationship with the United Church of Christ. The two denominations explored merger possibilities in the early 1980s, but decided instead to enter a partnership agreement in 1985. By 1989, the two churches entered "full communion" with one another. Since 1989, Disciples and the United Church of Christ have sought to find ways to share tasks in mission and ministry. They have entered into agreements that fully recognize one another's members and ministers. Their most successful joint endeavor came with the creation in 1995 of the Common Global Missions Board (CGMB). The CGMB is composed of twenty members named by each of the two denominations and six other members named from partner churches around the world. The board has responsibility for oversight of all mission activities for both Disciples and the United Church of Christ.

In 2009, approximately 150 persons held overseas appointments located in forty-four countries. In addition, Disciples maintain close ties with some 270 international partners in around seventy countries. The CGMB supports ministry among approximately 2.7 million indigenous Christians closely associated with Disciples work across the world. In addition, the board continues to work closely with the united churches (all of which have historical connections to Disciples or UCC mission work over the past one hundred-plus years) located in Japan, Hong Kong, Thailand, Philippines, Northern India, Jamaica, Britain, South Africa, China, and other parts of the world.

Disciples continue to provide significant leadership to the larger ecumenical movement. Since 2007, Michael Kinnamon has served as the General Secretary of the National Council of Churches of Christ, USA, the third Disciples-identified leader to do so. In 2001, a meeting of church leaders created a new ecumenical organization called Christian Churches Together in the USA. They hoped to create a space where mainline, evangelical, Pentecostal, Roman Catholic, and Orthodox church leaders could work together for the mission of the church. Richard Hamm, General Minister for the Disciples from 1993-2003, has served as the organization's first full-time Executive Director. Suzanne Webb, another Disciple, followed Michael Kinnamon in becoming the president of Churches Uniting in Christ, the successor organization to the Consultation on Church Union, a group of ten denominations, most of which have been in conversation with one another since 1962. Disciples leadership in the ecumenical movement remains fully committed and actively engaged.

In 1999, members of the groups sharing the Stone-Campbell heritage in North America began meeting "to develop relationships and trust within the three streams of the Stone-Campbell Movement through worship and through charitable and frank dialogue 'that the world may believe.'" The streams represented were Disciples, the Christian Churches and Churches of Christ (see Chapter Twelve), and the Churches of Christ (see Chapter Nine). Six members from each group met twice a year, calling themselves the Stone-Campbell Dialogue. In December 2001 the Dialogue produced a statement confessing the sin of their division and affirming the beliefs that they held in common. Since then, meetings have invited leaders and members of all the groups to join together for worship and discussion once each year in major cities where the three streams share strength in numbers.

Since its beginning, Dialogue meetings have considered topics of importance for all three streams. Examples include papers on the Lord's Supper and worship at Dallas in 2007, and global mission at St. Louis in 2008. The meeting in Cincinnati in March 2009, a decade after the first meeting was held there, provided a time of reflection about the past and future of the dialogue. When the group met again in November that year in Lexington, Kentucky, members decided to shift their emphasis "to a new phase of cultivating unity through mission and service." This produced a focus on finding ways to encourage local mission and service projects that can be shared across the streams of the Stone-Campbell Movement.

Carrying through on a vision created by the Stone-Campbell Dialogue in 2004, leaders of the three streams around the world hosted a "Great Communion" in 2009 in which members gathered to share the Lord's Supper on Sunday, October 4, the two-hundredth anniversary of the publication of Thomas Campbell's *Declaration and Address*. Scores of congregations across the nation, and in places like Australia, New Zealand, Brazil, and Kenya participated, joining Christians across the three streams in common worship services including a shared communion service.

Other examples of recent cooperation between the streams of the movement include the publication in 2004 of *The Encyclopedia of the Stone-Campbell Movement* (Eerdmans Publishing Company) and the beginning of a new world history. The encyclopedia provides a comprehensive resource for all persons related to the Stone-Campbell heritage. The global history project brings together fourteen historians representing the movement's streams to produce a book covering Stone-Campbell history across the world.

CONCLUSION

Disciples still prefer simply to be known as Christians. But over the course of two centuries, the Disciples' understanding of Christian witness and of the "one church" has taken note of the changing times, and changed with them. This is partly because Disciples have always believed that human history is meaningful. God has entered human time to make a difference. Disciples celebrate this fact at the communion table and in the baptismal waters, through their active engagement with the world as they seek to embody both God's love and justice, and in their insistence that the church is one.

When the Campbell congregations united with the Stone congregations on the frontier in 1832, the Disciples of Christ represented the cutting edge of ecumenical success in North America. As indicated in these pages, Disciples have been invested in unity talks and movements over the past century. None of these have involved formal unions, but the Disciples partnership with the United Church of Christ in North America has served as a new model for cooperation in mission between denominations.

Disciples have long emphasized that divisions are caused by human beings. Therefore, Disciples remain uncomfortable with division and continue to seek a way for the church to live into Christian unity. Disciples believe that unity rests in God because Christ is the head of the church. All Christians, by virtue of their relationship to Christ, are already members of God's church. The unity of the church is, therefore, actually a gift established by God in Christ, not something that human beings can establish through their own efforts. It is up to the church to represent faithfully the unity that already exists as a result of God's grace. Denominations

175

represent only a fraction of the church. The church contains all Christians and all denominations no matter how divided in history they might actually be.

The Disciples continuing quest for unity does not seek sameness of expression, or the denial of difference or diversity. Rather, it seeks to express the fullness and diversity of theologies and peoples as all Christians seek to serve God as members of one church. Diversity, for Disciples, is one of the great gifts God has given the church. As long as theologies, church structures, creeds, and other differences are used to keep the church from experiencing its oneness in God, Disciples are committed to find a way toward more visible expressions of unity. Alexander Campbell once declared, "We . . . should hang our Sectarian trumpets in the hall and study ecclesiastic wars no more." Disciples have not always succeeded in meeting that expectation, but their entire history is marked by an earnest desire to seek a renewal of Christian unity in the life of the church. And the work continues.

FOR FURTHER READING

Alvarez, Carmelo. *Sharing in God's Mission: The Evangelical Pentecostal Union of Venezuela and the Christian Church (Disciples of Christ) in the United States, 1960-1980*. Ph.D. diss., University of Amsterdam, 2006.

Brock, Rita Nakashima. *Journeys by Heart: A Christology of Erotic Power*. New York: Crossroad Publishing Company, 1988.

Brock, Rita Nakashima, Claudia Camp, and Serene Jones. *Setting the Table: Women in Theological Conversation*. St. Louis: Christian Board of Publication, 2006.

Brock, Rita Nakashima, and Rebecca Ann Parker. *Saving Paradise: How Christianity Traded Love of This World for Crucifixion and Empire*. Boston: Beacon Press, 2008.

Jiménez, Pablo A. *Somos Uno. Historia, teología y gobierno de la Iglesia Cristiana (Discípulos de Cristo)*. St. Louis: Chalice Press, 2005.

Jones, Serene. *Trauma + Grace: Theology in a Ruptured World*. Louisville: Westminster John Knox, 2009.

Cardwell, Brenda and William K. Fox. *Journey Toward Wholeness: A History of Black Disciples of Christ in the Mission of the Christian Church*. St. Louis: Board of Trustees of the National Convocatoin of the Christian Church, Christian Board of Publication, 1990.

Hopgood, William C. *Born Apart, Becoming One: Disciples Defeating Racism*. St. Louis: Chalice Press, 2009.

Jha, Sandhya. *Room at the Table: Struggle for Unity and Equality in Disciples History*. St. Louis: Chalice Press, 2009.

Machado, Daisy. *Of Borders and Margins: Hispanic Disciples in Texas, 1888-1945*. New York: Oxford University Press, 2003.

Miller-McLemore, Bonnie. *In the Midst of Chaos: Caring for Children as Spiritual Practice*. San Francisco: Jossey-Bass, 2007.

Stone-Campbell Dialogue. Materials can be found at the following website: http://www.disciples.org/ccu/programs/stonecampbell/

Toulouse, Mark G. "Muddling Through: The Church and Sexuality/ Homosexuality." In David Balch, ed. *Homosexuality, Science, and the "Plain Sense" of Scripture*. Grand Rapids: Eerdmans, Jr., 1999. See pages 6-41.

Yu, Guenee. "Asian American Disciples." In Douglas A. Foster, Paul M. Blowers, Anthony L. Dunnavant, and D. Newell Williams, eds. *Encyclopedia of the Stone-Campbell Movement*. Grand Rapids: Eerdmans, 2004. See pages 40-41. The *Encyclopedia* contains well-written articles of interest on virtually every subject covered in this book.

QUESTIONS FOR DISCUSSION

1. Disciples were among the first mainline denominations to ordain women, but Disciples history reveals a long struggle for women to find equal place within the denomination. As you think about this historical struggle, in what ways might this historical struggle help us to understand the difficult relationship between culture and faith as Christians form their beliefs and practices?

2. What does unity in the midst of diversity mean to you? How would you describe the source of Christian unity and in what ways might your congregation work to be faithful to a theological commitment to unity in the twenty-first century?

3. How might a commitment to Christian unity help Christians work through complicated and occasionally divisive social issues that often confront the life of the church?

Study Guide

General Comments on Teaching *Renewing Christian Unity*

1 This study guide is written for small groups or church classes. It assumes that each student or family has a copy of the book *Renewing Christian Unity: A Concise History of the Christian Church (Disciples of Christ)*, and has read the appropriate chapter before the class meets.

2 Some Christians do not see a need for studying church history and may even see it as negative. There are many reasons for this. One is that Disciples have been deeply influenced by the American idea that the past is something from which we need to escape so we can move to a better future. Some resist the idea that Disciples have been shaped by the ideas and events of their past, seeing our origins only in scripture. The first part of chapter one responds to such objections.

3 Goals for the study of the history of Disciples in *Renewing Christian Unity* include:

a. to help members of Disciples congregations understand more fully how they have been shaped by the people, ideas, and events of the past, especially the last two hundred years.

b. to explain and demonstrate the ideals that gave rise to Disciples in the nineteenth century and what we might draw from this heritage to strengthen our churches today.

c. to examine and evaluate the parts of our history that have been detrimental to our Christian health so we might change our patterns and live more faithfully.

4 The material in each chapter focuses on one main idea and has been kept to as manageable a level in both length and complexity as possible. Teachers may feel a need to do other background reading on each topic. The "For Further Reading" section at the end of each chapter lists materials that deal specifically with the

subject matter for that chapter. If you want to add four or five key books to your library that will consistently be helpful in this study, the following are ideal:

   a. Duane D. Cummins, *The Disciples: A Struggle for Reformation* (Chalice Press, 2009).
   b. Michael Kinnamon and Jan G. Linn, *Disciples: Reclaiming Our Identity, Reforming Our Practice* (Chalice Press, 2009).
   c. Mark G. Toulouse, *Joined in Discipleship: The Shaping of Contemporary Disciples Identity* (Chalice Press, 1997).
   d. Fran Craddock, Martha Faw, and Nancy Heimer, *In the Fullness of Time: A History of Women in the Christian Church (Disciples of Christ)* (Chalice Press, 1999).
   d. Douglas A. Foster, et. al., *Encyclopedia of the Stone-Campbell Movement* (Eerdmans, 2005).

5 This study is not merely to learn historical facts, but to help shape the faithfulness of the church and its members. Church historian Justo Gonzalez has said: "Every renewal of the church, every great age in its history, has been grounded on a renewed reading of history."

6 During the course of the study, classes might be opened and closed each week with prayer. The prayer might include the desire that this study will in fact be part of a process of formation that will renew and revitalize this church and Christ's church throughout the world.

CHAPTER 1: Disciples and History

Teaching/learning goals for this lesson include:

   a. Understand the nature of history and the Disciples approach to it.
   b. Point out and discuss ways the European and American backgrounds to the Stone-Campbell Movement helped shape it.
   b. Develop an appreciation for the debt Disciples owe to those who came before us.

    c. Identify strengths and weaknesses of the ideas and attitudes
we have inherited.

Lesson Plan

1. What is our understanding of the place of history in our lives?
   Does anyone present know people who tend to think of history
   as either "progress" (getting better and better) or as "decline"
   (spiraling downward)? For Christians who believe God stands
   behind creation, what might we think of the role history plays
   in our lives?
2. In what ways might Pelikan's understanding of the difference
   between tradition and traditionalism help us to think about the
   relationship of the Bible and church history to our lives as contemporary Christians?
3. In groups of two or three, can you talk about what you believe
   are the main ideas from the Protestant Reformation that have
   had a significant influence on what Disciples believe and practice today. After two minutes, can three or four of you offer
   your responses?
4. Chapter 1 focuses on the Lutheran, Zwinglian, Anabaptist, and
   Anglican (English) branches of the Reformation. One Lutheran
   legacy was to reject the Roman Catholic system of "penance"
   that implied people could merit or earn their salvation. Another
   was the insistence that "Scripture alone" was the source of
   what Christians believe and practice—not any creed, council,
   or Pope. **Group Discussion:** Why did the Lutherans emphasize
   these items? How have Disciples accepted these ideas or struggled with them?
5. One Zwinglian legacy not mentioned specifically in the book
   was the idea that only what is explicitly commanded by scripture can be practiced by the church—in other words, silence
   prohibits. In Zwingli's churches, therefore, there was no music
   or singing in worship since he believed there was no scripture
   that authorized such in worship. **Group Discussion:** This
   approach to scripture has created divisions within the Stone-
   Campbell Movement; how do you understand the authority of
   the Bible today?

6. One Anabaptist legacy was strict separation of church and state. That was the immediate reason for rejecting infant baptism—only those who have accepted and been saved by Christ are proper subjects for baptism, not everyone who is born into society. **Group Discussion:** How have traditional understandings of baptism among Disciples been like those of the Anabaptists? How different? Why?

7. One legacy of the Anglican Church was its claim to be a "Middle Way" [neither Catholic nor Protestant, but a New Testament church]. Many in the Anglican Church, however, believed it had not been fully "purified" of what they saw as Catholic corruption. These Puritans included several groups. All the early founding leaders of the Disciples came from one of those Puritan groups—the Presbyterians. That means at least two things: (a) they were Calvinists, and (b) they believed in church rule by "elders" (presbyters). **Group Discussion:** In what ways would you think the Presbyterian heritage of the early founding leaders of the Stone-Campbell Movement has shaped the Disciples?

8. All the influences we've looked at so far have been from the Protestant Reformation. The Enlightenment, partly a response to the antagonism and wars between religious groups that resulted from the Reformation, is a movement that emphasized human reason—some believed human reason could solve any problem. Some parts of the Enlightenment rejected Christianity as "un-reasonable." Yet other parts tried to make it more "reasonable." John Locke taught, among other things, that true Christianity was based only on the clear unmistakable teachings of the New Testament. Locke assumed that all reasonable persons would be able to agree on what the "express" teachings of the Bible were. **Group Discussion:** In your view, what are the positive aspects of this idea? What potential problems might be attached to this assumption?

CHAPTER 2: The Idea of Restoration in the Early United States
Teaching/learning goals for this lesson include:

a. Understand the ways the context of the United States helped to shape the Stone-Campbell Movement as it began.

b. Develop an appreciation for the contributions of Smith, Jones, and O'Kelly to Disciples.

c. Identify strengths and weaknesses of the ideas and attitudes Disciples have inherited.

Lesson Plan

1. The freedom prevalent on the frontier differed from the biblical idea of freedom, which emphasized freedom from selfishness to be able to serve others more fully. **Group Discussion:** Describe how these two notions of freedom differ from one another. What did freedom or "liberty" mean when applied to religion in the United States? What are some of the things that religious people wanted to be free from?

2. One thing people wanted to be free from was the old religious authorities. Many didn't want anyone telling them what to believe or practice—they could read the Bible and understand it for themselves. **Group Discussion:** What are the positive aspects of this attitude? When accompanied by a strong individualism, confidence in human reason, or the strength of popularity, what are the potential dangers in this attitude?

3. The idea of restoration implies that something has deteriorated or been altered to the point that it is not what it could be or ought to be. The idea also includes the belief that the church was somehow pure to begin with. Given that the church has always been a human institution, the idea of original purity may have its own innate problems. **Group Discussion:** What do you think the church has lost from the days of its earliest expressions? Are there elements of the church's life that have survived that you think ought to be changed? How might the church be understood as a changing institution? Is it possible for a church to adapt to changing contexts or cultures without abandoning its primary mission as church?

4. Two groups with roots in the American scene are the James O'Kelly Christians who broke with the Methodist Church, and the Elias Smith and Abner Jones Christians who broke with New England Baptists. **Group Discussion:** How do both of these groups reflect the three attitudes that characterized American Christianity? In what ways are these two groups

different from one another? In what ways are these groups like The Disciples in their beliefs, attitudes, and practices?

CHAPTER 3: Barton W. Stone and Christian Unity

Teaching/learning goals for this lesson include:

a. Describe the main events of the life of Barton W. Stone and his significance for the formation of the Stone-Campbell Movement.

b. Examine and analyze the events of the Cane Ridge meeting of August 1801 and how they affected the development of the movement.

c. Discuss the ideas of the "Last Will and Testament of the Springfield Presbytery" and how they have affected Disciples.

Lesson Plan

1. This chapter includes several references to historical facts about Stone's life and how these facts affected his approach to Christian faith. **Group Discussion:** What seems to have had the greatest influence on Barton Stone's experience of Christianity?

2. Barton W. Stone was the first of the reformers to lead a reform movement that became part of our immediate heritage as Disciples. His understanding of going back to the Bible was not simply an intellectual task to get the facts straight. The Bible to Stone was the living, active, word that transformed people and created a church that manifested the fruit of the Spirit (Galatians 5:22-23). **Group Discussion:** How might we understand the Bible to be a "living, active, word" today? How does the reader of the Bible, or the group who engages in its interpretation, interact with the words on the page? Can that act of interaction or resulting interpretation differ from age to age, person to person, or context to context?

3. One of the slogans that came from Stone was, "Let the unity of Christians be our polar star; let every Christian begin the work of unity in himself." Christian unity was central to Stone. **Group Discussion:** What influences do you think shaped

184

Stone's concern with Christian unity? What has influenced your own thinking with regard to Christian unity?

4. In 1803, Stone and four other ministers left the Presbyterian Church in the USA and formed their own Presbyterian body—the Springfield Presbytery. Yet by June of the following year they dissolved that body and committed to be simply Christians, rejecting non-biblical names and structures. The document they wrote, "The Last Will and Testament of the Springfield Presbytery," marks the first existence of any part of the Stone-Campbell Movement as a body separate from any other church. **Group Discussion:** Take a moment to re-read the "Last Will and Testament," found in these pages. As you read, mark phrases that sound familiar as things you have heard before in Disciples life. Mark as well any parts of the document that have *not* been part of your experience as Disciples. Discuss these things as a group.

CHAPTER 4: The Coming of the Campbells

Teaching/learning goals for this lesson include:

a. Examine and evaluate the ideas of Thomas Campbell in his *Declaration and Address of the Christian Association of Washington.*

b. Identify and analyze important life experiences of the Campbells that led them to begin their effort to reform the church.

c. Discuss the relationship of the Campbell churches to the Baptist associations.

Lesson Plan

1. The *Declaration and Address of the Christian Association of Washington, PA* is the second "founding document" of the Stone-Campbell Movement (after the "Last Will and Testament of the Springfield Presbytery"). The *Declaration and Address* is by far the longer document. The thirteen propositions of the document are included at the conclusion of this study guide. They form a small portion of the document. If you would like to look at the entire document, it can be found online at Hans

Rollmans' Web site: http://www.mun.ca/rels/restmov/texts/ tcampbell/da/DA-1ST.HTM. **Group Discussion:** As you read these thirteen propositions, mark phrases that sound familiar as things you have heard before in Disciples life. Mark as well any parts of the document that have *not* been part of your experience as Disciples. Discuss these things as a group. How do these propositions affect your own thinking about the unity of the church?

2. **Group Discussion:** Compare what you see in this small part of the *Declaration and Address* with what you saw last week in the "Last Will and Testament." What is the same? What seems to be different?

3. The Campbells were from Northern Ireland. They lived in the midst of religious and political antagonism between Protestants and Catholics. As members of the Church of Scotland, which was Presbyterian, they also were in the midst of various internal disputes. Each faction denounced the others, refusing to worship together or even recognize the others as Christians. **Group Discussion:** In groups of two or three, discuss for a few minutes instances of religious conflict you have personally experienced or that you know about. Share these in the larger group. As you talk about these instances of conflict, is there anything that you can pinpoint as the cause of religious conflict in general?

4. Alexander, Thomas's oldest son, arrived in America with the rest of the family in 1809 after an unsuccessful attempt to come the year before and a stay in Glasgow, Scotland. His experiences in Scotland with the divisive attitudes of the Presbyterians and the independents who had broken with the Presbyterians led him to many of the same conclusions his father had made. He readily joined his father's reform efforts. Alexander married Margaret Brown in 1811, and when their first child was born, the issue of infant baptism arose. This was not the first time he had thought of such matters. He had witnessed a division in Scotland among the followers of John Glas over the issue. But now he had to make a decision. Based on his study, he decided that infant baptism was not valid and that he needed to be immersed as a believer. The only other group that practiced believers' immersion was the Baptists. He persuaded a

186

Baptist minister to immerse him along with his wife, parents, sister, and two others. Not long afterward, the Redstone Baptist Association invited the Campbells' Brush Run Church to join the association. **Group Discussion:** Does this early affiliation with the Baptists surprise you? Are there still characteristics among Disciples that you would describe as close to the Baptists? In what ways do you think the eventual split with the Baptists affected the development of Disciples life?

5. The beginning years of the Stone-Campbell Movement were situated in a context seriously divided by race. **Group Discussion:** How did this racial conflict shape early Disciples? What kind of legacy have contemporary Disciples inherited because of the nineteenth and twentieth century racial and ethnic divisions?

CHAPTER 5: The Stone and Campbell Movements Unite

Teaching/learning goals for this lesson include:

a. Compare and contrast the ideas and beliefs of Barton W. Stone and Alexander Campbell and their movements.

b. Describe the process of uniting churches of the two movements, creating one of the largest religious reform movements in America.

c. Discuss how they were able to unite despite significant differences and what implications there are in this event for churches today.

Lesson Plan

1. There are seven classical categories of doctrine: God, Christ, Holy Spirit, Humanity, Salvation, Church, and Last Things/End of Time. **Group Discussion:** Using this list, can you describe doctrinal differences between Barton W. Stone and Alexander Campbell (a quick review of the chapter may help). Write down the differences identified by class members. Which of these differences seem most serious to you, and why?

2. The two groups also held beliefs in common. **Group Discussion:** What were some of the beliefs held in common

by the two groups? Are these beliefs still held in common by most Disciples?

3. The most famous early union of the Stone and Campbell churches took place in late December 1831 and early January 1832 in Lexington, Kentucky. Read part of the account of the union, especially parts of the speech of Raccoon John Smith and the acceptance by Stone of the proposal for unity. **Group Discussion:** What allowed the two churches in Lexington to come together in December, 1831? Why didn't their differences prevent this from happening? One major point to be made in this discussion is that union is never easy. Yet these people were so committed to living out their belief that there is one church that they could not easily drop it when difficult issues arose.

4. As this chapter indicates, unity has been important to the followers of both Christians and Disciples since their earliest days. **Group Discussion:** How strongly do you believe in the unity of the church? Upon whom does the unity of the church depend? Does it rest in God (and in the reality created by the work of Christ) or in the church? How is this commitment to the unity of the church expressed in your life, or in the life of your congregation?

CHAPTER 6: The Growth of the Stone-Campbell Movement

Teaching/learning goals for this lesson include:

    a. Name and analyze the things that contributed to the growth of the Stone-Campbell Movement before the Civil War.

    b. Evaluate the method of evangelism developed by Walter Scott.

    c. Describe the development of Disciples in Canada.

    d. Take note of the important role played by Disciples women in the nineteenth century.

Lesson Plan

1. Walter Scott began preaching what he called the *gospel restored* that could be made memorable by using five fingers to make his points (he started with six points—but five worked better): faith, repentance, baptism, forgiveness of sins, and the gift of

the Holy Spirit. **Class Discussion:** In what ways might Scott's five-finger exercise have been a welcome message to people on the frontier? In what ways might it have become a legalistic system of checking off things to do?

2. Literally hundreds of schools were formed by members of the Stone-Campbell Movement in the nineteenth and twentieth centuries. Almost all were liberal arts colleges—not schools to train professional ministers. The idea was that every Christian is a minister; therefore all students, regardless of major or chosen profession, should have a thorough education in scripture. **Class Discussion:** Do you agree with Alexander Campbell that every Christian is, in some sense, a minister? Why or why not? How are ministers educated today, and why do Disciples approach this education the way they do?

3. For most of our history the religious papers served one of the most important roles in giving Disciples a sense of connectedness. The statement "Disciples don't have Bishops, they have editors" reflects a truth about who wielded power in shaping Disciples identity among early Disciples. For Campbell, his papers and books (including the printed transcripts of his debates) served to get his ideas out to the widest possible audience. **Class Discussion:** How is Disciples identity shaped today? What might Disciples do to contribute more intentionally to this activity today?

4. Sometime after Disciples and Baptists split, Disciples faced the need to develop a more distinct method of cooperating with one another in the work of mission. **Class Discussion:** How did this work toward a cooperative impulse emerge among Disciples?

5. American culture during the nineteenth-century did not encourage the role of women in leadership. **Class Discussion:** How did church life and beliefs among Disciples enable women to claim their right to significant leadership in the church?

CHAPTER 7: Developing a Theology

Teaching/learning goals for this lesson include:

a. Define theology and understand that all Christians "do theology."

b. Identify some main areas of theological discussion and development in the churches of the Stone-Campbell Movement.

c. Discuss areas of theology that are major topics in Disciples today.

Lesson Plan

1. This chapter is about the theology of Disciples. **Group Discussion:** What does the term "theology" mean to you? How has the term been used (or not used) in church?

2. Theology is simply "thinking about God" or "thinking about faith," something that all Christians do by necessity—if we think at all. We can do it well, or we can do it carelessly and not very well. **Group Discussion:** What theological topics have you heard most emphasized in Disciples life. Write these on a chalkboard or whiteboard and try to analyze what patterns emerge. Do you see a focus on the unity of the church? Baptism? The Bible? Lord's Supper?

3. During the nineteenth-century, most Disciples assumed that God had created an unchanging church. Contemporary Disciples tend to recognize that the church is an historical institution that reflects a variety of cultures and contexts across the globe. **Group Discussion:** What implications for unity are present in this understanding of the church? How has our emphases on tolerance and diversity helped us to maintain our commitment to Christian unity.

4. Disciples believe strongly in the importance of reading the Bible. **Group Discussion:** How have we shifted our understanding of the Bible as revelation of God through our history? How has this affected our approach to the interpretation of the Bible?

5. Disciples have always emphasized the centrality of baptism. **Group Discussion:** Discuss Campbell's views on whether unimmersed persons could have a relationship with God. Why did he respond the way he did to the woman from Lunenberg when he believed so strongly in believers' immersion?

CHAPTER 8: The Great Divide of the Civil War
Teaching/learning goals for this lesson include:

   a. Examine ways the sectionalism of the Civil War and the accompanying racial attitudes shaped Disciples.
   b. Explain the role of the Civil War and sectionalism in the divisive issues of missionary societies and instrumental music in worship.

Lesson Plan

1. Moses Lard (originally pronounced "Laird") was one of the people most responsible for insisting that the Civil War had not divided the Stone-Campbell Movement. But, most certainly, the Civil War played a role in dividing Disciples from one another. **Group Discussion:** Why do you think the churches and leaders of the Stone-Campbell Movement took the positions they did regarding slavery? What role does culture play in shaping our theological perspective on questions like slavery and other social issues? The point of this exercise is to reveal how powerfully the surrounding culture affects the thought and actions of the church. Slavery was an accepted way of life for many Americans, and racial assumptions were shaped and developed by cultural contexts. Those who understood the Bible *primarily* as a book of facts to be handled in a legalistic manner defended slavery by reference to scripture. If one sees scripture *primarily* as the living, active word of God, which takes hold of our hearts and minds and seeks to transform us into Christians who represent the love and justice of God in the world (the gospel), then the practice of owning human beings will be seen for the inherently immoral practice it is and rejected by the church and Christians. All human beings are inherently the children of God whom God loves, regardless of race or any other human characteristic.

2. The Civil War revealed the sectional character of life in the United States. **Group Discussion:** Is it still true today? How have those sectional characteristics influenced Disciples of

191

Christ? How does racism fit into the historical picture for Disciples?

3. The connection between church and culture becomes especially clear in the Civil War. **Group Discussion:** In what ways do you think culture continues to influence Disciples today?

CHAPTER 9: Issues and Editors

Teaching/learning goals for this lesson include:

a. Describe some of the major issues and cultural factors that divided the Stone-Campbell Movement in the late nineteenth and early twentieth centuries.

b. Identify the complex nature of the divisive issues—that they were more than simply biblical/theological disputes.

c. Discuss the nature of the role of women in the societies and the early work developed by African-Americans and Latino/Latina Disciples.

d. Explain and evaluate the attitudes of division and unity embodied in Daniel Sommer and T. B. Larimore.

Lesson Plan

1. This chapter tells the story of division between the Christian Church (Disciples of Christ) and the Churches of Christ. **Group Discussion:** What do you know about the division that resulted in Churches of Christ and Disciples? Did you hear anything at all about the division when you were growing up? Did you know that the two churches were once the same movement?

2. As we saw in lesson eight, the sectional and racial attitudes of the post-Civil War era contributed powerfully to turning the "issues" usually given as the reason for the movement's division into divisive matters. Issues do not create division; people with divisive attitudes create division. **Group Discussion:** How did cultural factors connect to theological issues to create attitudes that led to division in the nineteenth and early twentieth century? How was the attitude of division present in both groups?

192

3. Daniel Summer and T. B. Larimore represent two different approaches to the developing differences among members of the Stone-Campbell Movement. **Group Discussion:** What did each group in the latter nineteenth century regard as fundamentally at stake in understanding the nature of the church and Christian unity that caused a church dedicated to unity to divide so dramatically?

CHAPTER 10: The Influences of Culture
Teaching/learning goals for this lesson include:

a. Describe some of the cultural and intellectual challenges that began to create a gap between Christians in the late nineteenth century.
b. Analyze a new understanding of Christian unity that developed in light of these challenges.
c. Describe the significance for Disciples of events like the World's Columbian Exposition and the Spanish-American War.
d. Identify the role played by Anglo-Saxon assumptions and how these assumptions shaped Disciples attitudes.

Lesson Plan

1. The turn of the century presented significant cultural and intellectual developments affecting all North American Christians. **Group Discussion:** How did these developments create new divisions among Christians?
2. Disciples leadership, during these years, began to articulate a new understanding of Christian unity connected to notions of civilization, race, and progress. **Group Discussion:** As you think about how culture affected the Disciples understanding of unity in the nineteenth century, how does this discussion help you to think more critically about the meaning of Christian unity today?
3. The disenfranchised groups (African-Americans, Native Americans, women, and others) struggled against cultural assumptions. **Group Discussion:** How did these groups

respond to these contextual factors? How did Disciples respond to the concerns of these groups?

4. The past three chapters have dealt in one way or another with cultural influences. **Group Discussion:** Take a few minutes and talk about the nature of the gospel. In your view, what is the good news of the gospel? Can you name more recent examples where Christians may be confusing cultural assumptions with the gospel?

CHAPTER 11: A New Theology

Teaching/learning goals for this lesson include:

a. Discuss the emergence of new developments in biblical interpretation and in theological understanding and their effects upon Disciples.

b. Examine the increasing emphasis on education among the Disciples.

c. Analyze the developing understanding of Christian unity and Disciples commitments to a variety of expressions within ecumenical Christianity.

Lesson Plan

1. Developments in theological and biblical interpretation affected Disciples profoundly during these years. **Group Discussion:** In what ways do you think these developments led to a revised, or perhaps even new, understanding of Disciples identity? Do you think Disciples identity is being revised in new and different ways today? What kinds of things influence these developments in self-identity?

2. Disciples seem always, since the days of their founding, to have taken education very seriously. **Group Discussion:** As you think about this historical commitment to education, how do you think it has affected the shape of Disciples life?

3. *Renewing Christian Unity* is a book that recognizes the importance of Christian unity as a compelling theme within Disciples history. **Group Discussion:** How did developments of the early twentieth century provide the possibility for new initiatives among Disciples in Christian unity? Have you been aware,

before reading this book, how many Disciples have fulfilled major roles as leaders in the ecumenical movement in both North America and across the world?

4. The concluding section of this chapter identifies at least three distinct forms of theological expressions developing among Disciples during the early twentieth century. **Group Discussion:** Do you see the residue of these forms existing within your experience of Disciples life today? If so, in what ways does it appear?

CHAPTER 12: A New Structure, New Mission, and New Division

Teaching/learning goals for this lesson include:

a. Examine the growth of Disciples at the turn of the century.

b. Describe the development of church polity among Disciples, particularly as it relates to their conventions, missionary societies, and finances.

c. Discuss the tensions that accompany these developments.

d. Understand the open membership controversy and its effects.

e. Explain the new theologies of both mission and church that emerged from these events, and the way they affected Disciples understanding of their life together in these areas.

Lesson Plan

1. As Disciples grew and matured, they found they had to deal with the practical questions of their life together with greater intentionality. **Group Discussion:** In what ways did the challenges posed by rapid growth and the desire to be effective within mission lead Disciples to create new ways of being the church together? What kinds of new challenges arose in the wake of new developments in church life?

2. The open membership controversy of the early twentieth century exposed somewhat an inability among Disciples to deal adequately with theological issues. **Group Discussion**: What theological arguments might have supported the practice of open membership on the mission field and also in the congregations

in North America? How did a theology of mission eventually emerge from these earlier difficulties and why did it encourage Disciples to drop the final "s" from the word "missions"?

3. Disciples engaged in a major effort to restructure the polity of the church during the 1960s, leading to the creation of the *Design* in 1968. **Group Discussion:** What role did theological understanding play in this effort? What kind of biblical metaphors helped them to think theologically about the nature of the church?

4. Disciples divided again during these years. **Group Discussion:** How would you describe the nature of this particular division? Are you familiar with congregations in your area who represent either the Churches of Christ or the Christian Churches and Churches of Christ? How does their understanding of the church and of the Christian life differ from yours or that of your own congregation of Disciples? Where might you find common ground?

CHAPTER 13: The Challenges Posed by Decline and Identity

Teaching/learning goals for this lesson include:

a. Analyze the trends affecting a decline in Disciples membership since about the 1960s.
b. Understand that Disciples of Christ have clearly entered the mainstream of the American cultural experience, but that the Christian tradition, increasingly, must not demand cultural priority or privilege.
c. Discuss the current challenges Disciples have faced within their church life.
d. Examine the Disciples response to numerical decline and other challenges.
e. Review the current statement of identity defining Disciples today.

Lesson Plan

1. Disciples, like other mainline church groups, have suffered serious membership decline since the 1960s. A significant number of cultural factors have contributed to this decline, but

a malaise within Disciples self-understanding has likely also contributed to it. **Group Discussion:** Since many of you have likely experienced some of this decline personally, what major factors would you cite that have contributed to it? What might your recipe be for "turning things around"?

2. Disciples have begun a number of initiatives to respond to their current context. **Group Discussion:** To what degree are you familiar with these initiatives? Which of them do you think hold the greatest degree of promise for the renewal and reinvigoration of Disciples of Christ church life?

3. Sharon Watkins has led Disciples to think more intentionally about Disciples identity. **Group Discussion:** How do you respond to these twelve marks of Disciples identity? Do they ring true for you? What might you say differently? What would you describe as the essence of Christian identity?

4. Disciples in North America exist within a cultural context that values diversity and religious pluralism. **Group Discussion:** How do you understand the mission of this church in this context? How might the cultural context cause you to define the meaning of Christian unity and contribute to the strength of its witness? In what ways might your congregation contribute to the development of dialogue and trust between Christianity and other religious faiths?

CHAPTER 14: Diversity in the Midst of Unity

Teaching/learning goals for this lesson include:

a. Explore diversity among Disciples.

b. Discuss the significant contributions and growth of congregations among African American, Hispanic, and Asian American Disciples.

c. Review the emergence of sexual orientation as an issue for North American churches, and the history of the question of ordination for gay and lesbian persons.

d. Analyze the modern ecumenical endeavors of Disciples.

Lesson Plan

1. This book has covered some of the difficulty faced by women among Disciples in fulfilling leadership roles in the church. **Group Discussion:** What is your experience of the leadership of women in the church? In what ways might the discussion about the role of women in the church illustrate the way cultural assumptions affect the life of the church?

2. The growth of ethnic congregations among Disciples of Christ has been a major factor in the increasing vitality of Disciples life in the last twenty years. **Group Discussion:** Reflect about the history of your congregation in the past twenty years. How does it compare with the increasing vitality of ethnic congregations during the same period? Are there ways you can imagine connecting your congregation's work to the ministry of other congregations in your city that might provide a model for how diverse congregations can work together as partners in mission?

3. The struggle for unity has provided a consistent theme throughout this book. **Group Discussion:** What do we mean when we describe unity as "a gift of God's grace"? How does this relate to our understanding that "divisions are caused by human beings"?

4. The diversity in the midst of Disciples has always meant that Disciples struggle with how to relate to a variety of social and cultural questions. **Group Discussion:** How might a commitment to Christian unity help Disciples maintain their connections to one another and others in the midst of social issues that some among them understand to be divisive? How do you understand the connection between a commitment to the gospel and a commitment to social justice? Does one demand the other, or are they independent from one another?

Thirteen Propositions from the
Declaration and Address of the Christian Association of Washington, PA

PROP. 1. That the Church of Christ upon earth is essentially, intentionally, and constitutionally one; consisting of all those in every place that profess their faith in Christ and obedience to him in all things according to the Scriptures, and that manifest the same by their tempers and conduct, and of none else; as none else can be truly and properly called Christians.

2. That although the Church of Christ upon earth must necessarily exist in particular and distinct societies, locally separate one from another, yet there ought to be no schisms, no uncharitable divisions among them. They ought to receive each other as Christ Jesus hath also received them, to the glory of God. And for this purpose they ought all to walk by the same rule, to mind and speak the same thing; and to be perfectly joined together in the same mind, and in the same judgment.

3. That in order to this, nothing ought to be inculcated upon Christians as articles of faith; nor required of them as terms of communion, but what is expressly taught and enjoined upon them in the word of God. Nor ought anything to be admitted, as of Divine obligation, in their Church constitution and managements, but what is expressly enjoined by the authority of our Lord Jesus Christ and his apostles upon the New Testament Church; either in express terms or by approved precedent.

4. That although the Scriptures of the Old and New Testaments are inseparably connected, making together but one perfect and entire revelation of the Divine will, for the edification and salvation of the Church, and therefore in that respect can not be separated; yet as to what directly and properly belongs to their immediate object, the New Testament is as perfect a constitution for the worship, discipline, and government of the New Testament Church, and as perfect a rule for the particular duties of its members, as the Old Testament was for the worship, discipline, and government of the Old Testament Church, and the particular duties of its members.

5. That with respect to the commands and ordinances of our Lord Jesus Christ, where the Scriptures are silent as to the express

time or manner of performance, if any such there be, no human authority has power to interfere, in order to supply the supposed deficiency by making laws for the Church; nor can anything more be required of Christians in such cases, but only that they so observe these commands and ordinances as will evidently answer the declared and obvious end of their institution. Much less has any human authority power to impose new commands or ordinances upon the Church, which our Lord Jesus Christ has not enjoined. Nothing ought to be received into the faith or worship of the Church, or be made a term of communion among Christians, that is not as old as the New Testament.

6. That although inferences and deductions from Scripture premises, when fairly inferred, may be truly called the doctrine of God's holy word, yet are they not formally binding upon the consciences of Christians farther than they perceive the connection, and evidently see that they are so; for their faith must not stand in the wisdom of men, but in the power and veracity of God. Therefore, no such deductions can be made terms of communion, but do properly belong to the after and progressive edification of the Church. Hence, it is evident that no such deductions or inferential truths ought to have any place in the Church's confession.

7. That although doctrinal exhibitions of the great system of Divine truths, and defensive testimonies in opposition to prevailing errors, be highly expedient, and the more full and explicit they be for those purposes, the better; yet, as these must be in a great measure the effect of human reasoning, and of course must contain many inferential truths, they ought not to be made terms of Christian communion; unless we suppose, what is contrary to fact, that none have a right to the communion of the Church, but such as possess a very clear and decisive judgment, or are come to a very high degree of doctrinal information; whereas the Church from the beginning did, and ever will, consist of little children and young men, as well as fathers.

8. That as it is not necessary that persons should have a particular knowledge or distinct apprehension of all Divinely-revealed truths in order to entitle them to a place in the Church; neither should they, for this purpose, be required to make a profession more extensive than their knowledge; but that, on the contrary, their

having a due measure of Scriptural self-knowledge respecting their lost and perishing condition by nature and practice, and of the way of salvation through Jesus Christ, accompanied with a profession of their faith in and obedience to him, in all things, [50] according to his word, is all that is absolutely necessary to qualify them for admission into his Church.

9. That all that are enabled through grace to make such a profession, and to manifest the reality of it in their tempers and conduct, should consider each other as the precious saints of God, should love each other as brethren, children of the same family and Father, temples of the same Spirit, members of the same body, subjects of the same grace, objects of the same Divine love, bought with the same price, and joint-heirs of the same inheritance. Whom God hath thus joined together no man should dare to put asunder.

10. That division among the Christians is a horrid evil, fraught with many evils. It is antichristian, as it destroys the visible unity of the body of Christ; as if he were divided against himself, excluding and excommunicating a part of himself. It is antiscriptural, as being strictly prohibited by his sovereign authority; a direct violation of his express command. It is antinatural, as it excites Christians to condemn, to hate, and oppose one another, who are bound by the highest and most endearing obligations to love each other as brethren, even as Christ has loved them. In a word, it is productive of confusion and of every evil work.

11. That (in some instances) a partial neglect of the expressly revealed will of God, and (in others) an assumed authority for making the approbation of human opinions and human inventions a term of communion, by introducing them into the constitution, faith, or worship of the Church, are, and have been, the immediate, obvious, and universally-acknowledged causes, of all the corruptions and divisions that ever have taken place in the Church of God.

12. That all that is necessary to the highest state of perfection and purity of the Church upon earth is, first, that none be received as members but such as having that due measure of Scriptural self-knowledge described above, do profess their faith in Christ and obedience to him in all things according to the Scriptures; nor, secondly, that any be retained in her communion longer than they continue to manifest the reality of their profession by their temper

and conduct. Thirdly, that her ministers, duly and Scripturally qual-
ified, inculcate none other things than those very articles of faith
and holiness expressly revealed and enjoined in the word of God.
Lastly, that in all their administrations they keep close by the observance of all Divine ordinances, after the example of the primitive
Church, exhibited in the New Testament; without any additions
whatsoever of human opinions or inventions of men.

13. Lastly. That if any circumstantials indispensably necessary
to the observance of Divine ordinances be not found upon the page
of express revelation, such, and such only, as are absolutely necessary for this purpose should be adopted under the title of human
expedients, without any pretense to a more sacred origin, so that
any subsequent alteration or difference in the observance of these
things might produce no contention nor division in the Church.

INDEX

203